Italian Delights

Christian
Teubner

Italian
Delights

BARRON'S

Woodbury, New York • London • Toronto • Sydney

First English-language edition published 1986 by
Barron's Educational Series, Inc.

© 1984 by Grafe und Unzer GmbH, Munich, West Germany

The title of the German edition is *Pizza and Pasta Variationen.*

All inquiries should be addressed to:
Barron's Educational Series, Inc.
113 Crossways Park Drive
Woodbury, New York 11797

Library of Congress Catalog Card No. 86-3454

International Standard Book No. 0-8120-5618-3

Library of Congress Cataloging-in-Publication Data

Teubner, Christian.
    Italian Delights.

    Translation of: Pizza und Pasta Variationen.
    Includes index.
    1. Pizza   2. Cookery (Macaroni)   I. Title.
TX770.T4813   1986   641.8'24   86-3454
ISBN 0-8120-5618-3

Color photographs by Christian Teubner

Translation by Tom Snow

PRINTED IN HONG KONG

6 7 8 9   9 8 7 6 5 4 3 2 1

CONTENTS

PREFACE

This cookbook will make it simple and fun to make the most delicious pizzas and pasta dishes. I have collected the best recipes I know and have tested every one for you. The color photographs are not just to enjoy looking at; they also provide serving and garnishing suggestions.

I have never enjoyed doing a book as much as I did this one on pizza and pasta. True, I am a pasta fan and especially an admirer of Italian cooking. So it was really an ideal opportunity for me to develop new ideas on this theme. It is of course hardly necessary anymore to boost Italian foods. Almost everyone has already discovered how good Italian food is—especially pasta and pizza dishes. I do hope, however, that when you try these recipes, you'll agree that they taste even better than what you've been served in restaurants anywhere.

Many pasta dishes and even many pizzas are very simple and quick to prepare. Still, the simplest foods are only at their best when prepared with fresh ingredients of the highest quality. And top-quality ingredients start with the pasta, which you really should try making yourself. Once you have been convinced of the superiority of homemade pasta, you will gladly take on the small amount of extra work to make your own pasta dough.

To make pasta-making as simple as possible, we've shown, in step-by-step photos, both how to make the dough and also the right way to fold and cut it. But if you don't have the time to make the pasta yourself and will be using prepared products, buy only the best quality. Many different shapes of outstanding quality are now offered in supermarkets and gourmet shops.

Selecting the other ingredients and making endless variations on the sauces are naturally also lots of fun. You will find a wide range of suggestions in this book. I start with what I feel are the greatest pizza recipes and follow up with several variations on spaghetti and recipes for homemade pasta, even whole-wheat pasta. Then come a lot of ideas for baked pasta dishes, including lasagne and cannelloni, and, last but not least, recipes for stuffed pastas like ravioli and tortelloni. Although fine tortelloni can be bought ready made, anyone who has ever prepared these delicious pockets of dough from scratch, starting with the pasta dough and ending with the filling, will always crave the pleasure of their full flavor again.

Now come the wonderful salads that can be made from pasta, as well as recipes for gnocchi, Italian dumplings. Finally, you will learn a little about the most important kinds of Italian cheeses, because without cheese (always freshly grated of course), pasta and pizza would not be the fabulous dishes they are. And it's nice to know that all ingredients are now available in supermarkets and gourmet food stores everywhere.

Enjoy leafing through this book and trying the recipes. Even more, enjoy tasting the results. Eating these delicious dishes will communicate something of the Italian joy of life to you, your family, and your guests.

BASICS OF PIZZA AND PASTA COOKERY

Thin sheets of dough were baked on hot stones as far back as prehistoric times. It is easy to imagine how pizzas developed little by little from those first baked breads. Archeologists have discovered that the Greeks and Romans were cutting thin sheets of dough into strips, creating foods that were not all that different from modern pastas. Some research has even been devoted to finding out who was the first to "discover" dried noodles. We know that the Arabs developed a method of coiling noodles around sticks to dry in the air, perhaps an explanation of why macaroni turned up first in southern Italy, especially Sicily. Pasta was known in Italy even before the legendary travels of Marco Polo to China. The Roman Marcus Gravius Apicius (born 25 B.C.) described a sort of lasagne boiled in a spicy broth in one of his two cookbooks. (Even though Marco Polo didn't contribute anything really new to Italian cookery with his Chinese noodles, the consumption of pasta dishes did become more and more popular in Italy from that time on.)

Another Italian world traveler, Christopher Columbus, brought back to Europe the ingredient that gave pizza and pasta much of their characteristic importance in Italian cuisine: the tomato. Although it took almost 200 years for tomatoes to come into popular use in Europe, the gift from the New World revolutionized Italian cooking, first in Naples, then all over Italy, then all over the world.

How to cook pasta al dente

The pot that pasta is cooked in must be very large. Use at least 1 quart (1 L) of water and 1 teaspoon of salt per 1/4 pound (100g) of pasta. Once the water is boiling, add the pasta and cover the pot. When the water boils again, stir once to prevent strands or pieces from sticking together. Boil the pasta, uncovered, until done.

The pasta should boil for from about 5 minutes for very thin shapes to about 15 minutes for thick rigatoni. It must be really *al dente*—slightly resistant to chewing—if it is to taste really good. Remove one strand every now and then and bite it. Remember that the pasta will continue to cook somewhat even in the serving bowl. When ready, pour the pasta into a sieve and drain well. Place in a preheated bowl and cover with a towel until you are ready to finish the dish.

The Tomato—Ingredient Number One

A highly flavored, fresh dark red tomato is preferable for both pizza and for tomato sauce. The so-called canning plum tomatoes, which are meaty and have a solid tomato flavor, are ideal but you could also use small, firm field tomatoes at the height of their season. The larger salad tomatoes are not very good for sauces or pizza toppings. If you can't get fresh tomatoes, peeled canned plum tomatoes are a good substitute.

Cheese—freshly grated

One of the most important ingredients in most pizza and pasta dishes is cheese. Grated cheese should always be freshly grated. The advantages are easy to understand—the freshness of a cheese is easier to determine when it is bought by the piece; it won't dry out as rapidly; when grated, a fresh cheese retains its flavor and texture.

PIZZA—ROUND AND RECTANGULAR

Focaccia with Tomatoes and Anchovies

The simplest type of pizza is a sheet of rolled-out bread dough with depressions punched into it and olive oil poured into the depressions. Coarsely ground salt is sprinkled over it and the dough is baked until really crisp. Here is a juicy version.

For 6 servings
Dough
2 1/4 cups (300 g) all-purpose flour
1 package active dry yeast
1/2 cup + 2 tablespoons (125 mL) lukewarm water
1/2 teaspoon salt
3 tablespoons olive oil
Topping
1 cup (100 g) green olives
1 3/4 cups (100 g) black olives
2 cups (450 mL) homemade tomato sauce (see pages 64 and 72)
16 anchovy filets
a few leaves of fresh oregano and basil
olive oil
salt
freshly ground black pepper

To make the dough, sift the flour into a bowl. Make a depression in the center and sprinkle the yeast into it. Dissolve the yeast in the water and cover with a light layer of flour. Let the yeast proof for about 15 minutes. Add the salt and olive oil and mix to form a smooth, soft dough. Dust the dough with flour, place in a greased bowl, cover with a towel, and let rise in a warm place for about 1 hour. The dough should about double in volume.

Punch down raised dough. Roll out to a uniform 1/4-inch (3/4-cm) thickness. Arrange it on a lightly greased baking sheet and perforate the top with a fork so that it won't blister while baking.

Pit and chop the olives. Spread the tomato sauce evenly over the dough and sprinkle with the chopped olives. Distribute the anchovy filets over the dough at regular intervals and sprinkle with the oregano and basil leaves. Let the pizza rise for another 15 to 20 minutes.

Preheat the oven to 425°F (220°C). Generously drizzle olive oil over the pizza. Bake on the middle rack of the oven for 20 to 25 minutes. Salt the pizza lightly, sprinkle with pepper, and cut into 24 rectangles. Serve at once as an appetizer or main course with other dishes.

Focaccia with Onions

For 4 servings
Dough
2 1/4 cups (300 g) flour
1 package active dry yeast
1/2 cup + 2 tablespoons (125 mL) lukewarm water
1/2 teaspoon salt
3 tablespoons olive oil
Topping
4 large yellow onions
5 tablespoons (75 mL) olive oil
salt and white pepper
1/2 cup (60 g) finely chopped bacon (optional)

Prepare the dough as described in the previous recipe and let it rise for 30 minutes, or until doubled in volume. Preheat the oven to 425°F (220°C). Peel and slice the onions in rings. Heat the olive oil in a pan and sauté the onion rings over low heat until they are translucent.

Punch down raised dough. Arrange the dough on a large lightly greased baking sheet and perforate it several times with a fork. Distribute the onion rings over the dough and sprinkle with salt and white pepper. The pizza won't be authentic, but it will taste very hearty if sprinkled with the chopped bacon. Let rise for about 20 minutes.

Bake the pizza on the middle rack of the oven for 20 to 25 minutes, then serve.

Pizza Margherita

They say this pizza was invented by a Neapolitan *pizzaiolo* (pizza baker) in honor of Queen Margherita of Savoy. The ingredients in this "patriotic" pizza reproduce the colors of the Italian flag: green basil, white mozzarella cheese, and red tomatoes.

The following recipe is for a pizza the size of a standard 12 x 16-inch (30 x 40-cm) baking sheet. It is enough for a between-meals snack or a small lunch for 4 people. It is also possible to bake small individual pies by dividing the dough into 4 portions.

For really small "party" pizzas the dough is divided into 12 portions. Each portion is then rolled out into a small round pie. The individual pies are treated and topped the same as the larger version, but the baking time is about 3 or 4 minutes shorter.

Dough
2½ cups (300 g) all-purpose flour
1 package active dry yeast
½ cup + 2 tablespoons (125 mL) lukewarm water
½ teaspoon salt
2 tablespoons olive oil
Topping
1 can (32 oz/850 g) peeled tomatoes
1 pound (1 kg) mozzarella
salt
freshly ground black pepper
10-12 fresh basil leaves
½ cup (125 mL) olive oil

Prepare the dough as described in the recipe for Focaccia with Tomatoes and Anchovies (page 8).

Photo 1: Although the dough can be mixed with the kneading attachment of a food processor or—as illustrated in the photograph—with a wooden spoon, the simplest way is by hand.

Photo 2: Punch down the raised dough. Roll out the dough to a uniform ½-inch (1½-cm) thickness on a floured surface and place on a lightly greased baking sheet.

Photo 3: Perforate the dough several times with a fork to keep it from blistering during baking.

Photo 4: To make the topping, drain the tomatoes in a colander, chop roughly, and distribute over the dough. Slice the mozzarella thin, and distribute slices over the surface.

Photo 5: Sprinkle salt and pepper over the pizza, then cover it with the basil leaves.

Let the pizza rise 10 to 15 minutes. Preheat the oven to 425°F (220°C).

Photo 6: Drizzle olive oil over the pizza and bake for 18 to 22 minutes on the middle rack of your oven. When ready, slice and serve.

Pizza with Vegetables

Pizza al verdure

For 4 servings
Dough
2¹/₂ cups (300 g) all-purpose flour
1 package active dry yeast
¹/₂ cup + 2 tablespoons (125 mL) warm water
¹/₂ teaspoon salt
2 tablespoons olive oil
Topping
1 medium onion
6 large fresh tomatoes
6 ounces (200 g) boiled ham
1 jar (6 oz/200 g) marinated artichoke hearts, drained
1 small zucchini
6 ounces (200 g) fresh mushrooms
2 ounces (100 g) black olives
1 teaspoon salt
freshly ground black pepper
6 ounces Italian fontina cheese
2-3 ounces (100 g) fiore sardo
2 tablespoons chopped fresh oregano
¹/₂ cup (125 mL) olive oil

Make pizza dough as described in the recipe for Focaccia with Tomatoes and Anchovies (page 8). Shape it in two balls, roll them out into ¹/₂-inch (1¹/₂-cm) thick rounds, place them on lightly greased baking sheets, and perforate each crust several times with a fork.

Peel and mince the onion and sprinkle over the pizzas. Wash the tomatoes, slice them thin, and distribute over the pizzas. Cut the ham into small cubes and sprinkle on the pizza.

Cut the artichoke hearts in halves or in quarters. Wash, dry, and slice the zucchini and mushrooms. Pit the olives and distribute them, along with the artichoke hearts, zucchini, and mushrooms, over the pizzas. Sprinkle with salt and pepper.

Slice the fontina thin and cover the pizzas with it. Grate the fiore sardo and sprinkle it over the pizzas along with the oregano. Let the pizzas rise 15 minutes.

Preheat the oven to 425°F (220°C). Drizzle the olive oil over the pizzas and bake on the middle rack of the oven for 20 to 25 minutes or until crust is golden brown.

Variation
Sfincioni

Dough
4 cups (500 g) all-purpose flour
1 package active dry yeast
1 cup (240 mL) lukewarm milk
1 large egg
¹/₂ teaspoon salt
Topping
2 pounds (1 kg) fresh tomatoes
3 garlic cloves, minced
3 medium onions
1 teaspoon salt
¹/₂ cup (125 mL) olive oil
1 cup (4 oz) black olives
1 tablespoon dried oregano
8 ounces (250 g) caciocavallo

Sift the flour into a bowl, make a depression in the center, sprinkle the yeast into it, and dissolve the yeast in the milk. Add the egg and the salt, beat into a smooth dough, cover, and let rise 20 to 25 minutes.

Peel the tomatoes, cut into pieces, and sprinkle the garlic over them. Peel the onions, slice into thin rings, and sprinkle them over the tomatoes. Add the salt and pour the oil over the whole mixture. This topping can be prepared several hours ahead of time; it will be even more savory after standing, covered, at room temperature for a few hours.

Preheat the oven to 425°F (220°C). Divide the dough in half, pull each piece out into a small round pie, and place each on a lightly greased baking sheet. Spread the tomato mixture over each pie. Pit and halve the olives and sprinkle them along with the oregano over the Sfincioni. Crumble the cheese and sprinkle over the pies.

Bake the Sfincioni on the middle rack of the oven for about 15 minutes or until the crust is brown and crisp. Drizzle a little olive oil over the pizzas and serve at once.

Calzone with Spinach

Calzone alla spinaci

This pizza with an "upper crust" is not only a very popular lunch but is also a between-meal snack when it is sliced in smaller portions.

For 4 generous servings
Dough
4 cups (500 g) all-purpose flour
1 package active dry yeast
1¼ cups (300 mL) lukewarm water
1 teaspoon salt
1 large egg
2 tablespoons oil
Filling
2 pounds (1 kg) fresh spinach
salt
1 medium onion
2 cloves garlic
4 tablespoons (60 mL) olive oil
freshly ground black pepper
6 ounces (200 g) boiled ham
½ pound (225 g) fontina cheese
½ cup (50 g) black olives
1 tablespoon capers
Glaze
1 egg yolk, lightly beaten

Prepare the dough as described in the recipe for Focaccia with Tomatoes and Anchovies (page 8).

Add the salt, egg, and oil, then mix to a smooth dough. Cover and let rise for another 40 to 50 minutes.

Pick through the spinach, remove the stems, and wash leaves well. Boil in salted water for about 5 minutes over high heat, then drain off the water. Drain, let the spinach cool, then chop it coarse. Mince the onion. Force garlic through a press.

Heat the olive oil in a large saucepan and sauté the minced onion and garlic over low heat until translucent. Add the chopped spinach and season with salt and pepper.

Cut the ham and cheese into small ¼-inch (¾-cm) cubes. Pit and mince the olives. Mix the cubes of ham and cheese, the olives, and the capers with the spinach.

Roll the dough out on a floured surface to double the size of a lightly greased 12 x 17-inch (30 x 42-cm) baking sheet. Cover the baking sheet with half the dough, letting the other half hang over the side. Perforate the dough in several places with a fork to keep it from blistering during baking. Spread the spinach mixture on the dough, leaving a margin of about 1 inch (2½ cm) uncovered. Spread the margin with the beaten egg yolk and fold the other half of the dough over the filling. Press the margins together. Let the calzone rise for 10 to 20 minutes before baking.

Preheat the oven to 425°F (220°C). Brush the top of the calzone with the rest of the beaten egg yolk and perforate top with a fork. Bake on the middle rack of the oven for 25 to 30 minutes, or until golden yellow.

Variation
Calzone with Onions

Prepare the same dough as for Calzone with Spinach.

To make the filling, peel 6 medium onions (700 g), slice into rings, and sauté in 5 tablespoons (75 mL) of olive oil over low heat until soft. Mix ¼ pound (250 g) cubed ham, 1 large egg, and 1 teaspoon salt with 2 tablespoons chopped fresh parsley and 6 oz (200 g) cubed provolone cheese. Stir into the cooled onions.

Preheat the oven to 400°F (200°C). Roll out the dough to twice the size of your baking sheet. Place the dough on the lightly greased sheet, and add the filling as described for previous recipe. Bake on the middle rack of the oven for 25 to 30 minutes or until golden yellow.

Pizza Provencale
Pissaladière

Pizza is not strictly Italian, as proved by *pissaladière*, a French-style pizza. It is from the region near Nice, a city with a Mediterranean cuisine.

For 6 to 8 servings
Dough
2 cups (250 g) all-purpose flour
1/4 pound (125 g) butter, softened
1/2 cup (125 mL) water
1 teaspoon salt
Topping
1 medium onion (preferably mild)
3 tablespoons olive oil
2-3 tablespoons water
1/2 teaspoon salt
1/2 teaspoon freshly ground black pepper
12 anchovy filets
2 medium tomatoes
1 cup (100 g) black olives
2 teaspoons bouquet de Provence (dried rosemary, thyme, basil, and oregano)

Sift the flour onto a countertop, make a depression in the middle, and slice the butter into it. Add the water and salt to the depression. Mix the butter with the water and flour, bringing the liquid from the center outward until all the ingredients are blended. Knead the dough a little and then cover. Let rest in the refrigerator for 1 to 2 hours. Meanwhile, mince the onion. Heat the oil in a pan and lightly sauté the onion until translucent. Add the water, sprinkle the salt and pepper over the mixture, and let onion cook over low heat for about 10 minutes.

Roll out the dough into a round pie crust about 14 inches (40 cm) in diameter. Line a 12-inch (32-cm) cake pan with the dough and push extra dough up the sides. Perforate the crust in several places with a fork, then distribute the cooled onion evenly over the dough. Arrange the anchovy filets on top of the onion in the form of a star.

Slice the tomatoes and pit and halve the olives. Distribute both uniformly over the pizza. Finally sprinkle the herb mixture over all.

Preheat the oven to 400°F (200°C). Bake the pizza on the middle rack of the oven for 30 to 35 minutes or until brown and crisp. Serve at once.

Variation
Onion pizza

Dough
2 cups (250 g) all-purpose flour
1 package active dry yeast
1/2 cup (125 mL) lukewarm milk
1/2 teaspoon salt
2 tablespoons (30 g) butter, softened
Topping
3 small onions
3 tablespoons olive oil
1/2 cup (125 mL) white wine
1/2 teaspoon salt
1/4 teaspoon freshly ground black pepper
20 anchovy filets
4 medium tomatoes
1/4 cup (100 g) black olives
1 tablespoon chopped fresh parsley
4 ounces (100 g) bacon, about 4 slices

Sift the flour into a bowl. Dissolve the yeast in the milk and mix into the flour along with the salt and butter. Mix the dough thoroughly, cover, and let it rise slowly, covered, in a cool place for 2 to 3 hours, or until doubled in bulk.

Peel and mince the onions and prepare as described for Pizza Provençale.

Preheat the oven to 400°F (200°C). Cut the bacon into small pieces. Roll out the dough, cover the baking sheet with it, and perforate several times with a fork. Distribute the onions over the dough and sprinkle with the bacon. Bake the pizza on the middle rack of the oven for 30 to 35 minutes, or until crisp. Serve.

Four Seasons Pizza

Pizza quattro stagioni

This is one of the classics of pizza, even though the ingredients change with the season. Usually it is a mixture of meat, fish, and vegetables.

For 8 servings
Dough
2¹/₂ cups (300 g) all-purpose flour
1 package active dry yeast
¹/₂ cup + 2 tablespoons (125 mL) lukewarm water
¹/₂ teaspoon salt
2 tablespoons olive oil
Topping
1 can (1 lb/500 g) peeled tomatoes
1 clove garlic
10 ounces (300 g) fresh mushrooms
1 jar (10 oz/300 g) mussels
2 jars (6 oz/175 g) marinated artichoke hearts
10 ounces (300 g) boiled ham
1¹/₂ cups (200 g) black olives
1 can (2 oz/60 g) anchovies
salt
freshly ground black pepper
1 tablespoon chopped fresh parsley
1 tablespoon chopped fresh oregano
1 teaspoon chopped fresh basil
1 pound (450 g) mozzarella
¹/₂ cup (125 mL) olive oil

Prepare the dough as described in the recipe for Focaccia with Tomatoes and Anchovies (page 8). When the salt and olive oil are added, beat to a smooth dough. Divide the dough in half and roll each half into a ball. Roll out the dough balls on a lightly floured surface into thin circles about 12 inches (30 cm) in diameter. Place circles on lightly greased baking sheets and perforate the dough in several places with a fork to keep it from blistering during baking.

Drain the tomatoes in a sieve and chop them coarse. Force the garlic through a press. Clean the mushrooms and cut them in half.

Distribute the tomatoes over the pies and sprinkle each with garlic. Mark the pizza in quarters with the tip of a knife. Top one quarter of the pizzas with the drained mussels and the artichoke hearts cut in halves or quarters. Slice the ham into strips and top the next quarter with it. Cover the third quarter with the mushrooms. For the final quarter, pit the olives, drain, and pat the anchovies dry; distribute over the remaining quarter of each pizza.

Sprinkle with salt, pepper, and half the chopped herbs. Cut the mozzarella into cubes and distribute over the pizzas. Sprinkle on the remaining herbs. Let the pizzas rise for 10 to 20 minutes.

Preheat the oven to 425°F (220°C). Drizzle the olive oil over the pizzas and bake on the middle oven rack for 20 to 25 minutes or until crisp and brown. After 10 minutes, drizzle a little more olive oil over the pizzas.

Hint: If you can't get fresh herbs, use dried ones. Just use half the amount called for.

Rustic Pizza with Ricotta

Pizza con ricotta

Even though most pizzas, especially the traditional ones, are made with a leavened dough, there is still a large number of other types, like Pizza Provençale (page 16) and the ones described on this page, that are made with unleavened dough. You can use cottage cheese instead of the ricotta. If you do, however, press it through a strainer or drain it in a colander.

For 6 servings
Dough
2³/₄ cups (350 g) all-purpose flour
¹/₂ cup (115 g) butter, softened
1 teaspoon salt
1 large egg
3 to 4 tablespoons water
Filling
10 ounces (300 g) ricotta or plain cottage cheese
3 large eggs
¹/₂ teaspoon salt
freshly ground white pepper
2 tablespoons minced fresh parsley
1 teaspoon chopped fresh marjoram
¹/₄ pound (100 g) provolone
¹/₄ pound (100 g) asiago
¹/₂ pound (200 g) salami or prosciutto, in one piece

Glaze
1 egg yolk, lightly beaten

Sift the flour onto a counter, make a depression in the center, and add the butter, salt, egg, and water to the depression. Rapidly knead the ingredients from the center out into the dry flour. Wrap the dough in foil and let rest in the refrigerator for about 30 minutes.

Stir the ricotta or cottage cheese in a bowl: add the eggs gradually. Season with salt and white pepper and mix in the chopped herbs. Cut the provolone and asiago into small cubes; likewise, cut the salami or ham into ¹/₄-inch (³/₄-cm) dice. Stir the cheeses and meat into the ricotta mixture.

Preheat the oven to 400°F (200°C). Cut off about ²/₃ of the chilled dough. On a lightly floured surface, roll out into a thin circle about ³/₄ inch (2 cm) in diameter. Line a lightly greased 10-inch (25-cm) round cake pan or springform pan with the dough and press the edges firmly against the wall of the pan. Slice off excess dough. Perforate the bottom in several places with a fork, then pour in the cheese mixture.

Roll the rest of the dough out to form an upper crust 10 inches (25 cm) in diameter. Brush the edge with beaten egg yolk, then cover the filling with the upper crust and press the edges together. Cut a 1-inch (2¹/₂-cm) hole in the center of the upper crust to let the steam escape.

Brush the pizza with the rest of the beaten egg yolk and bake on the middle rack of the oven for 45 to 50 minutes, or until golden on top.

Variation
Pizza with Onions

This pizza, with its mixture of ricotta, onions, and ham, is recommended for anyone who loves an onion pie. Follow the preceding recipe but decrease the amount of ricotta to 4 ounces (100 g) and replace with 1 cup (250 g) thinly sliced onions. Stir the eggs into the ricotta and cheese and add seasonings. Add the onions along with the cheese and ham. Bake as for original recipe.

Pizza with Artichokes

Pizza con carciofi

Although the topping for this pizza is very rich, what is special is the artichoke hearts. Although in Italy this dish is still often made with fresh artichokes, it is a lot easier to use canned artichoke hearts, which have been thoroughly drained.

For 4 servings
Dough
2¹/₂ cups (300 g) all-purpose flour
1 package active dry yeast
¹/₂ cup + 2 tablespoons (125 mL) lukewarm water
¹/₂ teaspoon salt
1 tablespoon (15 g) butter, softened
Topping
3 small ripe tomatoes
6 ounces (180 g) salami, sliced
2 jars (6 oz/175 g) artichoke hearts, drained and quartered
¹/₄ cup (120 g) black olives
¹/₄ pound (250 g) mozzarella
fresh oregano, basil, and a little rosemary
olive oil

Prepare the dough as described in the recipe for Focaccia with Tomatoes and Anchovies (page 8). Knead the dough vigorously on a floured surface for at least 5 to 10 minutes, beating it against the working surface from time to time to relax it and make it elastic. Cover and let rise for 30 minutes, or until doubled in bulk. Punch down dough and on a floured surface, roll out into two pizzas about 12 inches (30 cm) in diameter. Place each on a baking sheet. Perforate with a fork a few times to prevent the dough from blistering during baking.

Preheat the oven to 450°F (230°C). Blanch the tomatoes briefly in boiling water and strip off the skin. Cube and then distribute the tomatoes over both pizzas, leaving the edges of the dough uncovered so that the topping won't leak out during baking. Cover with the salami slices and add the artichoke hearts. Pit the olives and sprinkle over the pizzas.

Slice the mozzarella thin and distribute it over the pizzas. Sprinkle with the herbs and generously drizzle olive oil over the pizzas. Let dough rise 10 to 15 minutes.

Bake the pizzas on the middle rack of the oven until brown and crisp, about 15 to 25 minutes.

Variation
Pizza with Tomatoes and Artichoke Hearts

Make a leavened dough as described in the previous recipe. Divide in half and roll into two circles. Place circles on lightly greased baking sheets. Distribute 3 ounces (80 g) of chopped bacon over the top and cover with slices from 2 ripe tomatoes, 3 ounces (100 g) sliced canned mushrooms, and 6 halved or quartered marinated artichoke hearts. Season with salt and pepper. Distribute ¹/₂ pound (200 g) sliced mozzarella over the pizzas. Sprinkle with 1 teaspoon each of chopped fresh oregano and parsley. Drizzle ¹/₂ cup (125 mL) of olive oil over the pies. Bake at 400°F (210°C) on the middle rack of the oven for 20 to 25 minutes, or until golden brown.

Fresh Seafood Pizza

Pizza frutti di mare

Pizzas topped with seafood are especially delicious when fresh ingredients are available. It is unnecessary to use all the seafood called for in the recipe. A pizza made with mussels, fish, or shrimp alone will still taste outstanding. The layer of tomatoes is recommended as a basis in any case.

For 3 servings
Dough
2¹/₂ cups (300 g) all-purpose flour
1 package active dry yeast
¹/₂ cup + 2 tablespoons (125 mL) lukewarm water
¹/₂ teaspoon salt
2 tablespoons olive oil
Topping
1 can (1 lb/500 g) peeled tomatoes
1 clove garlic
1 whole snapper or porgy (or other firm-fleshed fish), about 1 pound (400 g)
3 calamari (squid)
salt
1¹/₂ pounds (600 g) mussels
¹/₂ pound (200 g) shrimp in the shell
freshly ground black pepper
1 tablespoon chopped fresh parsley
2 medium onions
1 bunch fresh basil (about 10 sprigs)
¹/₂ cup (125 mL) olive oil

Prepare dough as described in the recipe for Focaccia with Tomatoes and Anchovies (page 8). Add the salt and the olive oil and beat into a smooth dough. Cover and let the dough rise for another 20 minutes.

For the topping, drain the tomatoes in a sieve and then slice them coarse. Force the garlic through a press. Wash and clean the fish. Remove the head and tail. Slice the fish into strips, through the center bone. clean the calamari and boil about 10 minutes in salted water. Thoroughly clean the mussels under running water and steam in salted water until they open. Throw away any mussels that don't open. Remove the mussels from the shells. Shell and wash the shrimp. Drop into boiling water, cover, and immediately remove from heat. Let stand 2 or 3 minutes, then drain and cool.

Preheat the oven to 425°F (220°C). Divide the dough into 3 equal pieces and roll each into a ball. Roll out the balls of dough into thin circles on a lightly floured surface and place them on lightly greased baking sheets. Perforate the dough in several places with a fork.

Distribute the tomatoes over the pizzas. Sprinkle with the garlic, salt, pepper, and parsley. Slice the onions into rings, then arrange on pizzas. Add cooked and drained seafood. Distribute basil over the pies and add salt and pepper to taste.

Let the pizzas rise for 10 to 15 minutes, then drizzle the olive oil over them. Bake on the middle rack of the oven for 18 to 20 minutes or until golden.

SPAGHETTI VARIATIONS

Types of pasta: Pasta is made in an almost infinite variety of forms and lengths. Pictured here are some of the more common pastas usually available in supermarkets or fine food stores.

1 Gnocchi
2 Lasagna and green (spinach) lasagna
3 Spaghettini
4 Helical macaroni (*elicoidali*)
5 Spaghetti
6 Cannelloni and green cannelloni
7 Rigatoni
8 Large rigatoni (*grosso rigatoni*)
9
10 Macaroni of various diameters (*maccheroni, mezzani, bucatini*)
11

12 Tripolini
13 Ring macaroni—large (*anelli*)
14 Ring macaroni—small (*anellini*)
15 Trinette
16 Spaghetti sold in a coil (literally *chitarra,* "guitar")
17 Trenette
18 Green tagliatelle
19 Pennoni
20 Penne rigate (ridged *penne*)
21 Penne
22 Lumache ("snails")
23 Riso
24 Linguetinni
25 Conchiglie (literally "shells" of all sizes)
26 Tagliatelle
27 Fuselli
28 Fettuccine

Spaghetti with Croutons or Bread Crumbs
Spaghetti con la mollica

For 4 servings
5 slices (150 g) stale white bread
1/2 cup (125 mL) olive oil
8 anchovy filets
1 pound (400 g) spaghetti
salt
2 tablespoons minced fresh parsley
1/2 teaspoon salt
freshly ground white pepper

Crumble the bread or cut it into small cubes.

Heat half the olive oil in a pan and brown the bread in it, stirring constantly. Remove the bread. Add the rest of the oil and sauté the anchovies over low heat until they break up.

Cook the spaghetti in salted water until *al dente*. Drain well and place in a large warmed bowl. Sprinkle on the browned bread and then add the anchovies and oil. Sprinkle spaghetti with the parsley and season with salt and pepper. Toss well and serve immediately while the bread crumbs or croutons are still crisp.

Spaghetti Carbonara

Spaghetti alla carbonara

Carbonara is probably one of the simplest and best spaghetti dishes. Eggs and cream are Italian luxuries, but it's the bacon that makes the difference in this dish. Italians always use pancetta, a dry-cured unsmoked bacon, but you can substitute dry-cured ham or smoked bacon instead. If you use smoked bacon, its taste will change the flavor of the dish but it will be just as delicious.

For 4 servings
1/4 pound (120 g) pancetta or lean unsmoked bacon
1 medium onion
1/4 cup (50 g) butter or 4 tablespoons (60 mL) oil
1 pound (400 g) spaghetti
salt
2 large eggs
4 tablespoons (60 mL) heavy cream
freshly ground white pepper
2 ounces (50 g) pecorino
2 ounces (50 g) grana padano

Cut the bacon into small (1/4-inch/3/4-cm) cubes. Mince the onion. Melt the butter in a skillet, add the onion, and sauté lightly until soft. Add the bacon and heat for only 1 to 2 minutes, then remove it immediately from the stove.

Cook the spaghetti in plenty of salted water until *al dente*.

Mix the eggs with the cream, 1/2 teaspoon salt, and pepper in a large warmed bowl. Drain the spaghetti in a colander and add to the egg mixture while still hot.

Grate the cheeses. Pour the onion-and-bacon sauce and then the cheese on top of the spaghetti, toss carefully, and serve immediately.

Variation
Spaghetti with Olives and Oregano

This version is a very enticing variation on the carbonara recipe. The flavor of black olives harmonizing with the oregano goes extremely well with the taste of the day-cured meat. So prepare this dish only with pancetta or prosciutto.

Preparation is similar to the preceding recipe. Pit 1/4 cup (100 g) black olives, cut them in half or in quarters, and add them to the spaghetti along with 1 teaspoon minced fresh oregano and 2 teaspoons chopped fresh parsley.

Variation
Spaghetti with Boiled Ham

This is what might be called a milder version of Spaghetti Carbonara. It is prepared in the same way except that 1/4 pound (200 g) of diced boiled ham is used instead of the bacon. You could also replace all of the relatively sharp pecorino with grana padano.

Spaghetti with Mussels

Spaghetti con le cozze

Mussels and pasta complement each other, whether they are prepared plain or with tomato sauce.

For 4 servings
2 pounds (1 kg) mussels
1 medium onion
1 parsley root or bunch of parsley stems
1 medium carrot
1 stalk celery
2¹/₂ cups (600 mL) white wine
4 tablespoons (60 mL) olive oil
1 clove garlic, crushed
1 tablespoon chopped fresh basil
1 tablespoon chopped fresh parsley
salt
freshly ground black pepper
1 can (1 lb/500 g) peeled tomatoes, drained
1 pound (400 g) spaghetti
1 cup (100 g) butter, melted

Wash and scrub the mussels thoroughly, discarding any that are broken or already open. Quarter the onion. clean the parsley root and carrot and slice them lengthwise. Roughly chop the celery. Bring the root vegetables to a boil with 2 cups (450 mL) of the wine in a large pot. Add the mussels, cover, and steam for 10 to 12 minutes. By that time the mussels will have opened. Discard any that haven't.

Let the mussels cool a little, then remove them from their shells. Strain the broth and then place on stove and bring to a boil. Boil uncovered until reduced by half.

Heat the oil in a saucepan, briefly sauté the garlic, then add the herbs, ¹/₂ teaspoon salt, and pepper to taste. Add the tomatoes and mussel broth. Gently simmer the sauce over low heat for 30 minutes.

Add the mussels and remaining wine and continue to simmer sauce for 2 to 3 minutes.

Cook the spaghetti in salted water until *al dente*. Drain well, mix with the butter, and serve with the sauce.

Spaghetti with Clam Sauce

Spaghetti alle vongole e pomodori

For 4 servings
1 small onion
1 clove garlic
1 stalk celery
2 tablespoons oil
1 can (1 lb/500 g) peeled tomatoes
1 can (6 oz/175 g) minced clams
salt
freshly ground black pepper
¹/₂ tablespoon fresh oregano
¹/₂ tablespoon chopped fresh parsley
1 teaspoon fresh thyme leaves
¹/₂ cup (125 mL) white wine
1 pound (400 g) spaghetti
¹/₂ cup (80 g) freshly grated grana padano

Mince the onion and garlic. Chop the celery very fine. Heat the oil in a saucepan and add the onion, garlic, and celery. Stir in the tomatoes with their juice and cook 10 minutes over medium heat. Add the clams, 1 teaspoon salt, pepper, herbs, and wine. Simmer for 15 to 20 minutes over low heat, adding more liquid if necessary.

Cook the spaghetti in plenty of salted water until *al dente* and drain. Toss with the sauce and cheese and serve at once.

Spaghetti with Clams

Spaghetti alle vongole

This is one of the simplest and most elegant spaghetti dishes.

For 4 servings
1 clove garlic
2 or 3 shallots
1 medium carrot
1 stalk celery
1/2 cup (125 mL) olive oil
1 cup (240 mL) dry white wine
2 1/2 pounds (1 1/4 kg) small hard-shell clams, such as littlenecks
salt
freshly ground white pepper
1 tablespoon chopped fresh parsley
1 tablespoon each chopped fresh basil and lemon balm
1 pound (400 g) spaghetti

Force the garlic clove through a press. Mince the shallots very fine. Scrape the carrot and cut it into small cubes. Cut the celery into small cubes.

Heat the olive oil in a large saucepan. Briefly sauté the garlic and shallots, then add the carrot and celery and sauté for 2 to 3 minutes. Pour in the wine and set aside.

Scrub the clams under cold running water and add to the saucepan. Sprinkle with 1/2 tea-spoon salt and pepper to taste. Cover the pan and steam the clams for a few minutes until they open. Discard any that do not open. Add the minced herbs. Steam all the ingredients, uncovered, over low heat for another 10 to 15 minutes. The liquid will boil down to some extent.

Meanwhile, cook the spa-ghetti in plenty of salted water until *al dente*, then drain well. Place the pasta in a large bowl and pour the clam mixture on top. Mix well and serve immediately.

Hint: If possible, use the same wine to prepare the dish as you would to serve.

Variation Spaghetti with Fish Sauce

For 4 servings
1 pound (450 g) white fish filets, plus about 1 pound (450 g) fish tails and bones
1 medium carrot
1 stalk celery
1 parsley root or several parsley stems
2 tablespoons olive oil
1 clove garlic
1 medium onion, quartered
2 whole cloves
1 bay leaf
1 teaspoon salt
1 pound (400 g) spaghetti
1 tablespoon chopped fresh parsley

Wash and cut up the fish filets. Set aside. Rinse fish tails and bones. Clean and slice the carrot. Wash the celery and parsley root and chop them.

Heat the olive oil in a saucepan and lightly sauté the celery and parsley root. Add the garlic, onion, cloves, and bay leaf. Add the fish bones and tails, then cover with 6 cups (1 1/2 L) water. Simmer about 60 minutes, skimming off any foam. Pour through a sieve into another pot and simmer broth until reduced to about 3 cups (3/4 L).

Add salt and the spaghetti to broth. Boil for about 2 to 3 minutes, add the fish filets, and simmer another 8 minutes. Sprinkle with the parsley. Serve the spaghetti with bits of fish and a generous portion of sauce.

Spaghetti with Garlic and Oil

Spaghetti aglio e olio

This dish is an Italian standard. Although simple, its flavor is outstanding, making it a garlic lover's favorite. This is the southern Italian version, which is spicier because of the chopped red peppers.

For 4 servings
1 pound (500 g) spaghetti
salt
3 cloves garlic
1/2 cup (125 mL) olive oil
1 hot red pepper, minced
2 tablespoons chopped fresh parsley

Cook the spaghetti in salted water until *al dente*, then drain.

Force garlic through a press. Heat the olive oil in a pan, lightly sauté the garlic and chopped pepper, then pour over the hot spaghetti. Sprinkle the pasta with the chopped parsley and serve immediately.

Add cheese, if you like, but sprinkle on only the best, freshly grated Parmesan before serving.

Spaghetti with Garlic and Tomatoes

Spaghetti aglio e pomodori

For 4 servings
2 cloves garlic
4 tablespoons (60 mL) olive oil
salt
freshly ground white pepper
1 hot red pepper, minced
1 can (1 lb/500 g) peeled tomatoes
3 tablespoons chopped fresh parsley
1 pound (400 g) spaghetti
1 cup (100 g) freshly grated Parmesan cheese

Force garlic through a press. Heat the oil and lightly sauté the garlic, seasonings, and pepper. Add the tomatoes along with their juice and simmer the sauce until the tomatoes break apart. Add the chopped parsley.

Cook the spaghetti in salted water until *al dente*, then drain.

Serve the pasta with the sauce and sprinkle with grated cheese.

Variation Spaghetti with Garlic and Eggplant

For 4 servings
1 pound (500 g) eggplant
salt
2 cloves garlic
1/2 medium onion
1 red bell pepper
4 tablespoons (60 mL) olive oil
1 pound (500 g) spaghetti

Wash and peel the eggplant, then slice thin. Sprinkle with salt and let stand for 30 minutes. Crush the garlic cloves. Dice the onion half. Wash the pepper, cut it in half, and remove the stem and seeds.

Heat the oil in a pan, and lightly brown the garlic and onion. Add the pepper halves and sauté briefly.

Rinse the eggplant slices, pat dry, and sauté on both sides.

Meanwhile, cook the spaghetti in salted water until *al dente*. Drain.

Remove the pepper halves from the pan, add the spaghetti to the eggplant, and toss well. Serve at once.

Fried Spaghetti with Mussel Sauce

Spaghetti "usati" alle cozze

For 4 servings
3/4 pound (300 g) spaghetti
salt
1 medium onion
1 clove garlic
2 medium carrots
1/4 celery root
1 parsley root or several parsley stems
4 tablespoons (60 mL) oil
2 cups (450 mL) white wine
2 1/4 pounds (1 kg) mussels
freshly ground black pepper
1 pound (500 g) very ripe tomatoes
2/3 cup (80 g) butter
1 tablespoon chopped fresh parsley

Cook the spaghetti for about 8 minutes in salted water over high heat. Shake in a sieve to drain. Spread a baking sheet or porcelain platter with oil. Make 4 flat spirals of the drained spaghetti on the platter. Let them dry a little.

Mince the onion. Force the garlic clove through a press. Scrape the carrots and cut into small cubes. Peel the celery and parsley root and cut into small cubes.

Heat the oil in a large saucepan and sauté the onion, garlic, carrots, and celery and parsley root for about 8 to 10 minutes over low heat. Add the wine.

Scrub the mussels under cold running water, then add to the wine sauce. Season with salt and pepper, cover, and steam until the mussels open. Discard any mussels that don't open. Take mussels from shells and reserve.

Cut the tomatoes into large pieces and add to the mussel broth. Simmer 20 to 30 minutes, adding a little broth or water if necessary.

Strain the sauce through a fine sieve, add the mussels, cover, and simmer in the sauce for about 10 minutes.

Melt the butter in a skillet and brown the spaghetti nests on both sides until crisp. Do not crowd them; brown in 2 or more batches if necessary.

Serve the fried spaghetti sprinkled with parsley and with the mussel sauce on the side. Serve dry Orvieto wine as an excellent accompaniment.

Variation Spaghetti Casserole with Mussels

Briefly blanch the tomatoes in boiling water and remove the skins. Prepare a mussel sauce as in the preceding recipe but do not strain it.

Boil the same amount of spaghetti in salted water until al dente. Drain and mix with the mussel sauce in a large bowl. Add 1 1/2 cups (200 g) fresh peas and 1 1/4 cups (150 g) cubed fontina cheese.

Preheat the oven to 400°F (200°C). Butter a large casserole. Pour in spaghetti mixture and distribute the rest of the butter over the top in small pieces.

Bake the casserole on the middle rack of the oven for 30 to 40 minutes or until bubbly.

HOMEMADE PASTA

The recipes in this book can certainly be made with commercial pastas. When time is short it is a good idea to concentrate one's efforts on the sauce. Still, making your own pasta is a wonderful experience. Homemade pasta is especially delicious in simple dishes in which the flavor of the pasta itself is important— Spaghetti with Garlic or Fettuccine Alfredo, for example. Once you find that making pasta dough is not that difficult, you'll want to use your own pasta for most dishes.

Pasta is simple to make

The prerequisite to success in cooking is having fine ingredients. Don't compromise—the seasonings must be fresh, the vegetables, fish, or meat of the highest quality. So why not use the finest pasta, too?

Pasta is sold in a wide range of price and quality, and often it tastes quite satisfactory. Nevertheless, homemade pasta simply can't be beat. When people say they don't have the time to make their own pasta nowadays, they just haven't looked into it lately:

1. Preparation is very simple. Using as a rule of thumb, 1 egg, 1 tablespoon oil, and a pinch of salt for every 3/4 cup (100 g) of flour, you can make the dough in a jiffy (see basic recipe). It is also possible to use a food processor to make the dough.

2. Pasta looks harder to roll out and cut than it actually is. it goes very quickly. An inexpensive pasta maker can be used to roll and cut it.

3. Pasta dough can be made ahead of time whenever you have an hour free.

Basic Pasta Recipe

For about 1 1/2 pounds (680 g) pasta
2 1/2 cups (300 g) all-purpose flour
3 large eggs
1 teaspoon salt
3 tablespoons olive oil

Photo 1: Mound up the flour on a smooth surface. (A marble pastry board would be ideal.) Make a well in the center and drop the eggs into it.

Photo 2: Add the salt and olive oil.

Photo 3: Beat the salt and oil into the eggs with a fork, incorporating a little flour as well.

Photo 4: Push the rest of the flour toward the center of the well with both hands and blend with the egg mixture.

Photo 5: Knead the flour and eggs together little by little. If the dough gets too stiff to knead, add a little water and work it in.

Photo 6: Knead the dough on a floured surface for about 10 minutes, pressing it flat with the heels of the hands, folding it over, and pressing it flat again until it is smooth, glossy, and elastic.

Cover the dough and let it rest for 1 to 2 hours before working it further.

Making Pasta with a food processor

A food processor with a dough hook can be a big help in making pasta dough. Put the flour in the bowl along with the eggs, salt, and olive oil. Process with the dough hook until the dough turns into a solid mass. (If the dough becomes very stiff, gradually add a few spoonfuls of water.) Take the ball of dough out of the processor and knead on a floured surface until the dough is smooth and elastic. Cover dough and let rest 1 to 2 hours.

Rolling and cutting homemade pasta

Whether you use a pasta maker or roll out the dough with a rolling pin and cut it with a knife, there is no difference in quality, assuming that you cut your pasta thin enough.

Photo 1: Roll out the relaxed dough (dough that has rested at least 1 hour) in two thin portions on a lightly floured surface. Roll the pin alternately from left to right and from top to bottom so the dough is uniform.

Photo 2: Fold the dough. Dust the surface of the sheet with flour or, even better, with fine semolina. Fold it toward the middle from each end, like a letter.

Photo 3: Now cut the strips into desired width (fettuccine, for example, is 1/16 to 1/8 inch/4 to 5 mm). Spread strips loosely over a towel to dry.

Photo 4: Hand-operated pasta makers usually have two adjustable smooth rollers for rolling out the dough. The dough is shaped into a long strand as you crank it through the machine at the greatest possible width. Adjust the machine to a narrower width and crank the dough through again. Repeat until you get the desired final width.

Photo 5: Allow the rolled-out strips of dough to dry a little (but not too much because they will break) before cutting them with the machine. Pasta makers have either continuous rollers for each type of pasta or rollers of different widths. In the latter case, the unused part of the rollers is covered with a plastic shield and the strips of dough cranked through are cut to the desired width.

Photo 6: The finished pasta can now be dried. Let the pasta dry overnight before cooking or storing (for a few days).

Variation
Whole-wheat Pasta

This pasta has a more powerful flavor and sticks to the ribs longer.

For 1 pound (450 g)
2 cups (400 g) whole-wheat flour
1 tablespoon soybean flour
2 large eggs
2 teaspoons seasoned salt
3 tablespoons sunflower oil
5 tablespoons (75 mL) warm water

Mix the flours and heap up on a smooth surface. Make a well in the middle and put in the eggs, salt, and water. Make the dough like an ordinary pasta dough (adding a little more flour if it gets too soft) and knead until dough is springy and stops sticking to the surface. Shape into a ball, brush with a thin layer of oil, and let stand for 1 hour under a prewarmed bowl.

OTHER PASTA DISHES

Fettuccine Alfredo

This is a heroic instance of simplicity and exquisite flavor. It is also an example of how the finest ingredients lead to the best results. Use only homemade pasta.

For 4 servings
10 ounces (300 g) fettuccine
salt
1/4 cup (60 g) butter
1 cup (120 g) freshly grated parmesan cheese
1 cup (240 mL) cream
freshly ground white pepper
pinch of freshly grated nutmeg

Cook the fettuccine in plenty of boiling salted water until *al dente*. Drain well.

Melt the butter in a large saucepan and swirl the pasta through it quickly. Add the cheese and toss with two forks. Pour the cream on top and mix in well by constant tossing.

Season with salt, pepper, and a little nutmeg. Serve immediately.

Variation Fettuccine with Anchovies and Garlic

10 ounces (300 g) fettuccine
salt
2/3 cup (150 mL) olive oil
1 small hot red pepper
12 anchovy filets
2 cloves garlic, crushed
2 tablespoons chopped fresh parsley
1/4 cup (40 g) capers

Cook the fettuccine in plenty of salted water until *al dente*, then drain well.

Heat the olive oil in a pan. Cut the pepper in half, remove the seeds, and sauté in hot oil for about 2 minutes. Mince the anchovy filets and add to the pan along with the crushed garlic cloves. Sauté briefly, stirring constantly. Add the parsley and capers, stir well, and spread the mixture over the fettuccine. Serve immediately.

Variation Fettuccine with Herbs

This dish is quick to make and can be varied by using different herbs.

4 ripe tomatoes
2 medium onions
2 cloves garlic
4 tablespoons (60 mL) oil
2 tablespoons (30 g) butter
2 tablespoons chopped fresh herbs (parsley, basil, sage)
pinch of salt
freshly ground white pepper
1 pound (500 g) fettuccine
freshly grated parmesan cheese

Dip the tomatoes briefly in boiling water, peel, and cut in half. Squeeze out seeds and discard; dice tomatoes. Mince the onions and garlic cloves.

Heat the oil and butter and sauté the onion and garlic over low heat until translucent. Add the herbs and tomatoes, season with salt and pepper, and sauté lightly for 2 minutes

Cook the fettuccine in plenty of salted water until *al dente*, then drain and fold into the sauce. Serve sprinkled with the cheese.

Tagliatelle with Walnut Sauce

Tagliatelle al sugo di noci

For 4 servings
1¹/₂ cups (200 g) shelled walnuts
salt
freshly ground white pepper
10 fresh basil leaves
¹/₂ clove garlic, crushed
2-3 tablespoons heavy cream
1 cup (240 mL) olive oil
1 pound (400 g) tagliatelle
chopped fresh basil or parsley

Grind the walnuts until fine in a mortar or blender and season with ¹/₂ teaspoon salt and a pinch of pepper. Add the basil and garlic a little at a time and work into a smooth paste. Stir in the cream a little at a time until mixture is smooth.

Place the walnut paste in a large bowl and stir in the olive oil drop by drop with a hand-held electric mixer. This will take a fairly long time, but you must keep the sauce from separating.

Cook the pasta in plenty of salted water until *al dente*, then drain and rinse with cold water. Serve with cool sauce and sprinkle on the basil or parsley.

Tagliatelle with Zucchini

Tagliatelle con le zucchine

For 4 servings
1 pound (500 g) small zucchini
1 small onion
1 clove garlic
6 tablespoons (150 mL) olive oil
salt
freshly ground black pepper
1 teaspoon chopped fresh basil
2 teaspoons chopped fresh parsley
1 pound (400 g) tagliatelle
freshly grated parmesan cheese

Wash the zucchini and slice them about ¹/₄-inch (³/₄-cm) thick. Mince the onion and garlic.

Heat the oil in a pan and sauté the zucchini slices one portion at a time until they are slightly browned, about 6 to 8 minutes. Remove and set zucchini aside. Drain off 2 tablespoons of the cooking oil into a saucepan. Sauté the onion and garlic and add the zucchini. Add ¹/₂ teaspoon salt, a pinch of pepper, basil, and parsley and sauté 2 to 3 minutes over high heat.

Cook the pasta in plenty of salted water until *al dente*, then drain and serve with the zucchini. Sprinkle with the cheese.

Variation
Pasta Casserole with Zucchini

The preceding recipe can easily be converted into an excellent casserole. Butter the inside of a casserole and fill it with alternating layers of pasta and zucchini prepared as described above. Mix ¹/₂ cup (50 g) of grated parmesan cheese with ¹/₂ cup (50 g) of bread crumbs and 1 tablespoon of chopped fresh parsley and sprinkle them over the top. Dot with 2 tablespoons (50 g) of butter cut into small chunks and bake in the middle of the oven at 400°F (200°C) for 15 minutes.

Pasta with Shrimp

Tagliatelle con i gamberetti

For 4 servings
1 pound (400 g) tagliatelle or fettuccine
salt
10 ounces (300 g) fresh small shrimp in the shell
1 cup (240 mL) heavy cream
freshly ground white pepper
1 tablespoon chopped fresh parsley

Cook the pasta in plenty of salted water until *al dente*, then drain well.

Boil the shrimp 2 to 3 minutes in salted water, pour off the water, and shell the shrimp.

Place cream in a saucepan over medium heat and cook for about 6 to 8 minutes or until reduced by about 1/3. Add the shrimp. Season with salt, pepper, and parsley, then simmer for another 5 to 6 minutes.

Mix the sauce with the pasta and serve immediately.

Pasta with Tomato-Shrimp Sauce

Tagliatelle del cardinale

For 4 servings
1/2 cup (100 g) butter
1 clove garlic, minced
8 ounces (200 g) shelled shrimp
1 cup (240 mL) puréed tomatoes
salt
freshly ground black pepper
6 tablespoons (150 mL) dry white wine
1 tablespoon chopped fresh parsley
1 pound (400 g) tagliatelle
3/4 cup (80 g) freshly grated parmesan cheese

Melt the butter in a skillet and sauté the garlic over low heat. Add the shrimp and sauté 2 to 3 minutes over high heat, stirring constantly. Add the puréed tomatoes, 1/2 teaspoon salt, pepper, and wine, then stir in the parsley. Simmer 15 to 20 minutes over low heat.

Cook the pasta in salted water until *al dente*, then drain well.

Pour the shrimp sauce over the pasta. Serve the cheese on the side.

Variation
Fettuccine with Peas and Shrimp

1 large onion
2 tablespoons (30 g) butter
2 cups (250 g) shelled peas
1/2 cup (125 mL) fish or meat broth
salt
freshly ground white pepper
4 ounces (150 g) jumbo shrimp, cooked and shelled
1/2 cup (125 mL) heavy cream
1 tablespoon chopped fresh parsley
1 pound (400 g) fetuccine
freshly grated parmesan cheese

Mince the onion very fine.

Melt the butter in a skillet and sauté the onion over very low heat until transparent. Add the peas and broth and season with salt and pepper. Simmer about 10 minutes.

Cut the shrimp in thick slices and add to sauce. Simmer for about 4 to 5 minutes over low heat.

Blend in the cream, add the parsley, and continue to simmer for 2 or 3 more minutes.

Cook the pasta in salted water until *al dente*, then drain and mix with the shrimp. Serve immediately.

Trenette with Basil Sauce

Trenette al pesto

Although pesto, the famous Genoese basil sauce, is obtainable all along the Riviera, it is supposed to have been merchants from Genoa who contributed to its invention. That's why the Genoese swear that they're the only ones with the real recipe. This most popular of all pasta sauces goes best with trenette.

For 4 servings
4 cloves garlic
1/2 cup (50 g) pine nuts
salt
2 cups (120 g) fresh basil leaves
1/2 cup (50 g) grated pecorino cheese
3/4 (80 g) grated parmesan cheese
1/4 teaspoon freshly ground black pepper
1 cup (240 mL) extra-virgin olive oil
1 pound (400 g) trenette

Slice the garlic cloves thin, then pound them fine in a mortar along with the pine nuts and 1 teaspoon of salt. (You could also use a food processor or blender.) Wash the basil leaves, pat them dry, chop, and add to the nut paste. Blend all the ingredients to make a creamy paste. work in the cheeses. Finally, mix in the pepper and olive oil. If you want a slightly milder pesto, use parmesan cheese alone instead of a mixture of parmesan and pecorino.

Cook the trenette in plenty of salted water until *al dente*. Drain well. Mix the pesto and pasta, and serve immediately.

Hint: Pesto can also be prepared ahead of time and frozen. Follow this recipe but use only 2 garlic cloves, half the amount of salt, and no cheese. Add just enough olive oil to keep the paste moist. Put the pesto in an airtight plastic container and freeze. Before using, thaw pesto and blend in 2 more garlic cloves, the rest of the salt, and then add the cheese.

Variation
Trenette with Onion Sauce

3 medium onions
4 ounces (120 g) boiled ham
4 sage leaves
1/4 cup (50 g) butter
salt
pinch each of sugar and ground black pepper
1 cup (240 mL) beef broth
1 cup (240 mL) heavy cream
1 pound (400 g) trenette
3/4 cup (80 g) freshly grated parmesan cheese

Dice the onions and the ham. Wash the sage leaves and dry well.

Melt the butter in a skillet, add the onions and sage, and sauté about 20 minutes over low heat; the onions should not brown. Season with salt, sugar, and pepper. Add the broth. Simmer the sauce about 12 to 15 minutes over low heat.

Cook the pasta in salted water until *al dente*, then drain well.

Stir the cream and ham into the onion mixture and simmer a few minutes longer. Serve the sauce over the pasta. Sprinkle with the freshly grated parmesan.

Trenette with Seafood

Trenette frutti di mare

This delicious dish could well be the first course of an elegant meal serving eight. The particular combination of seafoods you select will depend on what happens to be in the market. The essential here is that everything be absolutely fresh.

For 4 servings
2 medium carrots
1 stalk celery
1 parsley root or several parsley stems
2 tablespoons oil
2 cups (450 mL) water
4 small calamari (squid)
4 sea scallops
12 ounces (350 g) trenette or fettuccine
8 cooked medium shrimp
4 cooked langoustines or 1 lobster tail
1/3 cup (80 g) butter
Sauce
2/3 cup (150 mL) heavy cream
4 ounces (120 g) gorgonzola cheese
freshly ground white pepper
pinch of freshly grated nutmeg

Clean the carrots, celery, and parsley root and slice fine.

Heat the oil in a large saucepan and lightly sauté the cubed vegetables for 4 to 5 minutes. Add the water and bring to a boil. Simmer the calamari in the broth for 5 to 7 minutes or until tender.

Place the scallops in a slotted spoon and hold them in the boiling broth for about 2 minutes.

Slice the scallops and calamari.

Cook the trenette in salted water until *al dente*, then drain well.

Shell the shrimp and remove langoustines or lobster meat from the shells. Heat the butter in a skillet and sauté the shrimp, langoustine or lobster meat, and scallops until golden brown, about 2 minutes.

To make the sauce, pour the cream into a saucepan set over medium heat and cook down by about half. Stir in bits of the cheese with a small whisk, then season with white pepper and a little nutmeg.

Arrange the hot pasta on the plates, add the sautéed seafood, and cover with the gorgonzola sauce.

Variation
Baked Pasta with Seafood

The same recipe can be transformed into an exquisite first course when baked in scallop shells.

Thickly butter 8 scallop shells and construct a small nest of pasta in each. Fill the nests with the sautéed seafood and cover with the cheese sauce. Add a little freshly grated parmesan and a few dots of butter on top. Bake the shells on the middle rack of the oven at 400°F (200°C) for about 5 to 10 minutes.

Pasta with Bolognese Sauce

Pasta col ragù alla bolognese

This is certainly the most famous Italian dish next to pizza. When Italian pasta is the subject, it is this hearty meat sauce everyone thinks of.

For 4 servings
1 small onion
1 medium carrot
1 stalk celery
1/2 parsley root or several parsley stems
2/3 cup (80 g) butter
10 ounces (300 g) lean ground beef
1/2 cup (125 mL) beef broth
2 tablespoons tomato paste
1/2 can (8 oz/250 g) peeled tomatoes, drained
salt
freshly ground black pepper
1 tablespoon minced fresh parsley
1 teaspoon fresh thyme
1 teaspoon fresh basil
1/2 cup (125 mL) red wine
1 pound (400 g) tripolini
3/4 cup (80 g) freshly grated grana padano or parmesan cheese

Mince the onion. Clean the carrot, celery, and parsley root, and slice very thin.

Heat the butter in a large saucepan. Lightly sauté the vegetables in the butter, then brown the ground beef over very high heat. Add the broth, tomato paste, and tomatoes and season with salt, pepper, parsley, thyme, and basil. Bring to a boil, cover, and simmer over very low heat for 40 to 50 minutes

Add the wine, and simmer 5 to 10 minutes longer.

Cook the pasta in salted water until al dente, then drain well. Serve the pasta with the sauce and grated cheese.

Variation Spinach Pasta with Bolognese Sauce

An outstanding variation on this classic dish is to serve the sauce with spinach pasta. Prepare the sauce with 1 bay leaf, 1 clove, and 1 chopped garlic clove. Stir in 1/2 cup (125 mL) heavy cream and let the sauce stand for a few minutes to blend the flavors and thicken slightly. Remove the bay leaf and clove before serving. Pour over spinach noodles. Sprinkle with freshly grated parmesan cheese.

Macaroni and Cheese

Maccheroni ai quattro formaggi

That pasta and cheese go extremely well together has been known for ages. Two different cheeses are often used together in Italy—parmesan and mozzarella, for example. The following recipe calls for four different cheeses and makes a delectable dish. If served as a first course these quantities will be enough for 6 to 8 portions.

For 4 servings
3 ounces (80 g) provolone
3 ounces (80 g) fontina
3 ounces (80 g) caciocavallo
1/2 cup (125 mL) milk
salt
1 pound (500 g) macaroni
1/4 (60 g) butter
1/2 (60 g) freshly grated parmesan cheese
chopped fresh parsley

Grate or cut the first three cheeses into small pieces in a bowl. Heat the milk just to the boiling point and pour over the cheeses. Let the mixture of cheese and milk stand for 30 minutes.

Meanwhile, bring salted water to a boil and cook the macaroni for 10 to 12 minutes or until *al dente*. Drain well.

Melt the butter in a large, deep pan and toss the macaroni in it. Pour the milk and cheese mixture over it, and add the grated parmesan. Heat until the cheese melts, then serve immediately, sprinkled with chopped parsley.

Variation Macaroni with Gorgonzola

7 ounces (200 g) gorgonzola cheese
1/2 cup (125 mL) milk
1/2 cup (125 mL) crème fraîche
salt
freshly ground white pepper
1 teaspoon minced hot red pepper
1 pound (400 g) macaroni

Very carefully slice the rind off the gorgonzola and cut the cheese into small cubes. Add to a pot along with the milk and heat slowly over low heat until the cheese melts. Gradually stir in the crème fraîche to make a creamy paste. Season with salt, white pepper, and red pepper.

Cook the macaroni in salted water until *al dente*, then drain well. Add the macaroni and mix well. Serve immediately.

Macaroni with Sardine Sauce

Pasta con le sarde

This elegant pasta sauce comes from Sicily, specifically from Palermo. It uses ingredients that have been available to Sicilians for ages. The original recipe calls for wild fennel, but it can be replaced by the domestic variety available in supermarkets. Although this sauce goes with any pasta, it is best with a tubular form.

For 4 servings
10 ounces (300 g) fresh fennel (1 small head)
salt
4 1/2 cups (1 L) water
1 medium onion
2 anchovy filets
1 pound (400 g) fresh sardines
2 tablespoons extra-virgin olive oil
salt
freshly ground black pepper
pinch of saffron
1/4 cup (25 g) raisins
1/4 cup (25 g) pine nuts
1 pound (400 g) macaroni

Wash the head of fennel and boil in lightly salted water until soft, about 20 minutes. Drain, preserving the water, and wrap in a towel. Squeeze out the rest of the water, then mince the fennel. Mince the onion. Slice the anchovy filets thin. Remove the heads, backbones, and tails from the sardines and slice the fish into small pieces.

Heat the oil in a skillet and lightly sauté the onion until translucent; stir in the sliced anchovy filets, add the sardines and the fennel. Season with the salt, pepper, and saffron. Add the raisins and pine nuts. Simmer for about 10 minutes.

Meanwhile, cook the macaroni in the fennel cooking water until al dente, then drain. Mix the macaroni with the sauce and heat gently for a few minutes over low heat to blend flavors.

Variation
Macaroni Casserole

A very tasty casserole, also serving four, can be made from the same recipe. Generously butter a large casserole. Line the bottom with cooked macaroni and cover with the sardine sauce. Add alternating layers until all the ingredients have been used (macaroni on top). Sprinkle the casserole with 3/4 cup (100 g) of grated caciocavallo and dot with butter. Bake for 15 minutes at 425°F (220°C) on the middle rack of a preheated oven.

Pizza Maker's Pasta

Mezzani alla pizzaiola

This recipe comes from southern Italy. There is a steak dish in Naples called *bistecca alla pizzaiola*, in which the meat is stewed in a sauce reminiscent of pizza. Using thin slices of meat instead of steak results in a sauce that is an ideal complement to pasta.

4 servings
1 pound (400 g) mezzani or macaroni
salt
1 pound (400 g) beef filet or prime rib
1 clove garlic
1/2 onion
1/4 cup (30 g) capers
3 tablespoons olive oil
freshly ground black pepper
1 tablespoon chopped fresh parsley
1 teaspoon chopped fresh oregano
1 can (1 lb/500 g) peeled tomatoes
3/4 (80 g) freshly grated parmesan cheese

Cook the mezzani or macaroni in salted water until *al dente*, then drain. Keep warm, covered, in a slow oven.

Slice the beef thin and cut in small pieces. Mince the garlic clove and onion. Chop the capers. Heat the olive oil in a skillet and sear the beef on both sides over very high heat. Do not crowd; brown meat in several batches if necessary. Add the garlic, capers, onion, seasonings, and herbs.

Drain the tomatoes, chop them roughly, and add to the beef. Braise 6 to 8 minutes at medium heat. Serve the meat and sauce with the pasta sprinkled with parmesan.

Variation
Macaroni Pizzaiola with Mushrooms

Once the meat has been seared, add 8 ounces (250 g) of sliced button mushrooms or, even better, chanterelles. Proceed as in the foregoing recipe.

Variation
Macaroni Casserole Pizzaiola

This basic recipe can easily be transformed into a hearty casserole. The ingredients are almost the same; just use some olive oil to grease the baking dish and have 8 ounces (200 g) mozzarella sliced. Cook the macaroni until *al dente*, drain very well, and put about 1/3 of it in the casserole. Place about half the sauce on top, spreading it well, then add half the sliced mozzarella. Add another third of the pasta, another layer of sauce, the remaining slices of cheese, and finally the last of the macaroni. Sprinkle the top with grated parmesan cheese and olive oil. Bake the casserole at 400°F (200°C) on the middle rack of the oven for about 20 minutes or until bubbly.

Pasta with Saffron and Fennel

Pasta col finocchio

For 4 servings
10 ounces (250 g) fresh fennel
4 tablespoons (60 mL) olive oil
1 large onion, minced
1/2 clove garlic, crushed
1/2 cup (50 g) chopped almonds
1/2 cup (50 g) pine nuts
1/4 cup (30 g) dried currants
salt
freshly ground white pepper
2-3 tablespoons dry white wine
1/4 teaspoon saffron
1 pound (400 g) penne

Clean the fennel and cook in lightly salted water until tender, about 20 minutes. Remove and cool, reserving the cooking water. Slice the fennel into small cubes.

Heat the olive oil in a skillet and brown the onion and garlic. Add the almonds, pine nuts, currants, and fennel. Season with salt and pepper. Last, add the wine and simmer 3 or 4 minutes.

Dissolve the saffron in the water left from cooking the fennel. Heat the water to a boil and boil the pasta until *al dente*, about 12 to 15 minutes. Drain well in a colander. Mix the pasta with the vegetable sauce in the skillet, heat briefly, and serve immediately.

Hint: Buy only a little saffron at a time, not just because it's one of the most expensive seasonings in the world but also because it doesn't keep its flavor very long.

Variation
Bucatini with Asparagus

For 4 to 6 servings
1 pound (400 g) bucatini
1 pound (400 g) fresh asparagus
3 medium tomatoes
6 tablespoons (75 mL) olive oil
salt
freshly ground white pepper
freshly grated parmesan cheese

Cook the bucatini in lightly salted water until *al dente*, about 12 minutes, then drain well.

Peel the asparagus (if necessary) and slice the spears into sections about 1 to 2 inches (4 to 5 cm) long. Blanch the tomatoes briefly in boiling water, strip off the skins, and cut into small cubes.

Heat the olive oil in a saucepan, add the asparagus and tomatoes, and sprinkle with salt and a lot of pepper. Braise for about 8 to 10 minutes, uncovered. Add the bucatini and reheat. Sprinkle with parmesan cheese and serve immediately.

Variation
Trenette with Cauliflower

Break 1 medium cauliflower into florets and wash. Cook the cauliflower in salted water until it is just cooked through; drain. Mince a small onion. Heat 2 tablespoons of oil in a pan with 1 tablespoon (15 g) butter. Sauté the onion until pale yellow. Add the drained cauliflower and season lightly with pepper. Add 3/4 cup (8 g) of pine nuts and 1/2 cup (50 g) of raisins and briefly sauté together. Boil 1 pound (500 g) of trenette or similar pasta in salted water until *al dente*, drain, and serve mixed with the cauliflower sauce.

Pasta with Tomato Sauce

Penne rigate con salsa napoletana

For 4 servings
1 pound (400 g) penne rigate or other tube pasta
salt
2 ounces (80 g) boiled ham
2 tablespoons olive oil
1 can (1 lb/500 g) peeled tomatoes
2 cloves garlic
1 red or green bell pepper
1/2 cup (60 g) pitted black olives
1 tablespoon chopped capers
4 anchovy filets
2 tablespoons chopped fresh parsley
1/2 tablespoon chopped fresh basil
1 teaspoon sugar
freshly ground black pepper
1/2 (125 mL) dry red wine
3/4 cup (80 g) freshly grated grana padano or parmesan cheese

Cook the pasta in salted water until *al dente*, then drain well.

Cut the ham into small 1/4-inch (3/4-cm) cubes.

Heat the olive oil in a large heavy skillet and lightly sauté the ham. Slice the tomatoes into large pieces and add them with the liquid from the can. Cut the bell pepper in half, removing the ribs and seeds. Dice fine, and add to the skillet. Force the garlic through a press into the frying pan and add the olives and capers. Sauté over low heat for 10 to 12 minutes. Chop the anchovy filets and add to the tomato sauce along with the parsley, basil, salt, pepper, and sugar. Add the wine and simmer 5 to 8 minutes longer. Serve the sauce on the pasta. Sprinkle with the grated cheese.

Tomato Sauce

Salsa di pomodori

This is a simple tomato sauce but it is outstanding as a basis for variations. Add ham, seasonings, or other ingredients that will contribute to its range of flavors.

For 2 1/4 cups (575 mL)
1/2 medium onion
1 clove garlic
2 1/4 pounds (1 kg) ripe tomatoes
5 tablespoons (75 mL) olive oil
2 teaspoons salt
2 teaspoons freshly ground black pepper
1 tablespoon chopped fresh parsley

Mince the onion and crush the garlic. Chop the tomatoes. Heat the oil in a heavy skillet and sauté the onion and garlic a few minutes over low heat, about 4 minutes. Add the tomatoes. Season with the salt, pepper, and parsley. Simmer the sauce, uncovered, over medium heat until thickened, about 30 minutes, stirring often. If desired, put sauce through a ricer to strain out seeds and skins.

Pasta Casserole

The basic tomato sauce can be used in an outstanding casserole. Select tube pasta like macaroni or small pasta like penne and add 8 ounces (250 g) of lean ground beef instead of ham. Then proceed as in the recipe for Pasta with Tomato Sauce.

Preheat the oven to 400°F (200°C). Mix the pasta with the sauce and place in a large buttered casserole. Sprinkle with grated cheese and dot with butter. Bake about 20 minutes on the middle rack of the oven.

Bucatini with Mushrooms and Tomatoes

Bucatini con funghi e pomodori

For 4 servings
1 pound (400 g) bucatini
salt
12 ounces (350 g) fresh button or wild mushrooms
1/2 cup (100 g) butter
freshly ground black pepper
1/2 medium onion, minced
1 can (1 lb/500 g) peeled tomatoes
2 tablespoons chopped fresh parsley
1 cup (100 g) freshly grated grana padano or parmesan cheese

Cook the bucatini in the salted water until al dente, and drain well.

Carefully clean the mushrooms and slice them thin.

Melt the butter in a large saucepan, add the mushrooms, and season with salt and pepper. Add the minced onion.

Sauté the mushrooms about 5 minutes at medium heat. Drain the tomatoes and force them through a sieve. Add the resulting purée to the mushrooms and simmer about 15 minutes at medium heat. Sprinkle with the parsley.

Serve the mushrooms with the bucatini and freshly grated cheese.

Bucatini with Wild Mushrooms

Bucatini con i funghi

For 4 servings
1 pound (400 g) bucatini
salt
1 pound (400 g) fresh wild mushrooms (chanterelles, cepes, shittake, or other)
4 tablespoons (60 mL) olive oil
1 clove garlic
1/2 cup (125 mL) beef broth
freshly ground black pepper
1 tablespoon minced fresh parsley

Cook the bucatini in salted water until al dente and drain well.

Carefully clean the mushrooms and slice if necessary so all pieces are about the same size.

Heat the oil in a heavy skillet. Slice the garlic paper thin. Add it and then the mushrooms to the oil, and sauté slowly over low heat. In about 5 minutes pour in the beef broth. Season with salt and pepper and sprinkle with parsley.

Mix the mushrooms with the hot bucatini and serve.

Variation
Pasta Casserole with Ham

As with other pasta dishes, this bucatini dish can easily be made into a delicious casserole. The tomatoes keep it especially juicy and the ham contributes special flavor. Prepare the above recipe, then rub the inside of a large casserole with butter. Fill casserole with alternating layers of bucatini-sauce mixture and 8 ounces (225 g) chopped ham. Sprinkle the surface with a mixture of the grana padano and parsley and dot with butter. Bake on the middle rack of the oven for about 20 minutes at 400°F (200°C).

OVEN AND STOVETOP CASSEROLES

Lasagna with Prosciutto

Lasagna al prosciutto

This casserole tastes especially good when the lasagne is boiled in beef broth instead of water. Use only a mild dry-cured ham such as prosciutto, because any pronounced smoky flavor would overpower the dish.

For 4 servings
8 ounces (200 g) lasagna
8¹/₂ cups (2¹/₂ L) beef broth
¹/₃ cup (75 g) butter, softened
4 ounces (150 g) dry-cured ham, such as prosciutto
4 ounces (150 g) mozzarella
4 large eggs
1 cup (100 g) freshly grated parmesan or grana padano
salt
freshly ground black pepper
bread crumbs

Cook the lasagna in all but ¹/₂ cup (125 mL) of the beef broth until *al dente*, about 10 to 12 minutes. Drain in a colander.

Generously coat the inside of a large casserole with butter.

Cube the ham and mozzarella. Mix the eggs with the grated cheese, ham, and mozzarella in a bowl. Season the remaining beef broth, salt, and pepper and stir broth into the egg mixture.

Preheat the oven to 400°F (200°C). Fill the casserole with alternating layers of lasagna and the ham, egg, and cheese mixtures, beginning with the lasagna and continuing until all the ingredients are used up. Cover the surface with a thick layer of bread crumbs and dot with butter. Bake on the middle rack of the oven for 30 to 35 minutes, or until bubbly.

Macaroni Omelet

Frittata di pasta

This recipe is an outstanding example of how to use leftovers. Although other types of pasta can be used, the dish is especially flavorful when made with hearty macaroni.

For 4 servings
1 pound (500 g) cooked long macaroni or other pasta, cooled
4 large eggs
6 ounces (180 g) freshly grated grana padano
¹/₂ teaspoon salt
freshly ground white pepper
1 tablespoon chopped fresh parsley
¹/₂ cup (120 g) butter

Slice the macaroni into sections about 2 to 3 inches (5 to 6 cm) long. Place the eggs in a bowl and add the cheese, salt, pepper, and parsley. Mix well.

Melt half of the butter in a 10-inch (25-cm) skillet. Distribute half the macaroni in the skillet and pour half of the egg and cheese mixture over the macaroni. Cook very slowly over low heat. Lift the edge of the omelet carefully with a knife to see if the bottom is brown. Turn carefully with a spatula onto a plate and then slide omelet back into pan to cook on the other side. Add a little more butter to pan if necessary and cook until the bottom is crisp and light brown.

Slide the omelet onto a plate. Cook the second omelet similarly.

This recipe is easy to vary by adding finely cubed ham or chopped and lightly sautéed onion and green bell pepper.

Spinach Lasagna, Bologna Style

Lasagna verdi all bolognese

For 4 servings
Dough

6 ounces (150 g) fresh spinach
salt
2¹/₂ cups (300 g) all-purpose flour
3 large eggs
2 tablespoons oil

Filling

2 ounces (60 g) bacon, about 2 slices
1 pound (500 g) lean ground beef
¹/₂ cup (60 g) each minced celery, carrot, and onion
1 teaspoon salt
freshly ground black pepper
1 tablespoon chopped fresh parsley
2 cups (¹/₂ L) beef broth
1 can (32 oz/850 g) peeled tomatoes

Béchamel sauce

2 tablespoons (30 g) butter
2 tablespoons all-purpose flour
2 cups (¹/₂ L) milk
¹/₂ teaspoon salt
freshly ground white pepper
freshly grated nutmeg
¹/₂ cup (80 g) freshly grated parmesan cheese

Pick through the spinach, wash and steam in the water clinging to the leaves for about 5 minutes. Drain, squeeze well, and force through a fine sieve. Sift the flour onto a working surface. Add the spinach and the other dough ingredients and prepare a pasta dough (see page 41). Add a little more flour or cold water if necessary. Let the dough rest, covered, at least an hour in the refrigerator.

Roll the dough out into strips the width of your casserole with a rolling pin or pasta machine. Cook the lasagna in plenty of salted water until *al dente*. Drain in a sieve.

Dice the bacon for the filling and brown in a saucepan. Add the ground meat and sear at high heat. Add the vegetables, season with the salt and pepper, and stir in the parsley. Pour in the broth and simmer 20 minutes over medium heat.

Add the tomatoes with their liquid and simmer the sauce over low heat for about an hour. The liquid should be almost completely boiled away.

To make the Béchamel sauce, melt the butter in a saucepan, add the flour, and stir 2 to 3 minutes over low heat. Gradually pour in the milk and whip with a whisk until the sauce is smooth. Season with salt, pepper, and nutmeg. let the sauce boil gently while stirring constantly, then simmer 20 to 30 minutes over low heat.

Preheat the oven to 400°F (200°C). Cover the bottom of the casserole with some of the meat sauce. Distribute some of the lasagna over it and pour some of the Béchamel sauce on top. Repeat until all the ingredients are used up, ending with a layer of Béchamel sauce. Sprinkle with the parmesan cheese and bake about 20 minutes on the middle rack of the oven until the top is golden brown.

Cannelloni

This stuffed pasta takes a little time to make from scratch, but the ready-made pastas are very convenient; they can be cooked in vigorously bubbling salted water for just 5 to 7 minutes.

If you have the ambition to make cannelloni yourself, roll out pasta dough (see page 41) very thin, cut into 4-inch (9-cm) squares, let them dry out a little, and then cook until quite *al dente.* Spread the squares out on a working surface, cover with filling, and roll up.

For 4 servings
Filling
2 tablespoons oil
1/2 medium onion, minced
1 clove garlic, crushed
4 ounces (100 g) chicken livers
10 ounces (300 g) lean chopped beef
8 ounces (250 g) fresh spinach
2 tablespoons (30 g) butter
1 teaspoon salt
freshly ground black pepper
1/2 teaspoon dried oregano
1/2 teaspoon dried basil
2 large eggs
2 tablespoons aged pecorino cheese
freshly grated Romano cheese
Béchamel sauce
2 tablespoons (30 g) butter
2 tablespoons all-purpose flour
1 cup (240 mL) milk
1/2 teaspoon salt
freshly ground white pepper
Tomato sauce
2 tablespoons olive oil
1 cup (100 g) minced onions
1/2 clove garlic, crushed
1 can (1 lb/500 g) Italian plum tomatoes
1/2 teaspoon sugar
1/2 teaspoon salt
fresh basil
2 tablespoons freshly grated parmesan cheese
2 tablespoons (30 g) butter

Cook the cannelloni, in vigorously boiling salted water until *al dente,* about 5 to 10 minutes.

Heat the oil in a large skillet and lightly sauté the onion and garlic. Chop the livers fine and add to the pan along with the ground beef. Sear at high heat, stirring constantly, for 5 to 6 minutes. Put the liver-meat mixture in a bowl and set aside.

Clean the spinach and blanch 1 to 2 minutes in hot water. Drain thoroughly. Chop the spinach coarsely.

Melt the butter in a pan, add the spinach, and season with the salt, pepper, oregano, and basil. Cook the spinach at high heat while stirring constantly for 4 to 5 minutes and add it to the liver-meat mixture. Add the eggs and cheese and mix well. Stuff the cannelloni with this mixture.

To make the Béchamel sauce, melt the butter in a saucepan, add the flour, and stir until smooth. Pour in the milk and add the salt and a little pepper. Stir the sauce vigorously with a whisk. Reduce the heat and simmer the sauce 2 to 3 minutes longer, stirring constantly, until it thickens.

To make the tomato sauce, heat the olive oil in a large saucepan and sauté the onion and garlic lightly until translucent. Slice the tomatoes thin and add them along with their liquid to the onion mixture. Season with the sugar, salt, and basil, washed and chopped coarse. Let the sauce boil up vigorously and simmer 30 to 40 minutes at low heat.

Preheat the oven to 400°F (200°C). Pour half of the tomato sauce into a large casserole, add a layer of cannelloni, and pour half of the Béchamel sauce on top. Add another layer of cannelloni and cover with the remaining tomato and Béchamel sauces. Sprinkle with the parmesan cheese and dot with butter.

Bake on the middle rack of the oven until the cheese melts and browns, about 20 minutes.

Cannelloni with Wild Mushrooms

Cannelloni con funghi

For 4 to 6 servings
Dough
2¹/₄ cups (300 g) all-purpose flour
3 large eggs
1 teaspoon salt
3 tablespoons olive oil
Filling
1 medium onion
1 medium carrot
1 stalk celery
4 tablespoons (60 mL) oil
8 ounces (250 g) wild mushrooms, such as cepes, chanterelles
10 ounces (300 g) ground beef
8 ounces (200 g) boiled ham
1 teaspoon salt
¹/₄ teaspoon freshly ground black pepper
1 tablespoon chopped fresh parsley
1 teaspoon chopped fresh marjoram
1 cup (240 mL) beef broth
1 large egg
¹/₂ cup (125 mL) sour cream
1 cup (100 g) freshly grated asiago cheese
¹/₄ cup (60 g) butter

Make a pasta dough from the flour, eggs, salt, and oil as described on page 8. Wrap in foil or plastic and let it rest at least an hour in the refrigerator.

Roll the dough out thin and cut into 4-inch (9-cm) squares. Let it dry briefly, then cook in vigorously boiling salted water for about 5 minutes. Drain.

To make the filling, clean, peel, or scrape the vegetables and dice fine.

Heat 2 tablespoons of oil in a heavy skillet. Sauté the onion, carrot, and celery until soft. Clean and slice the mushrooms, add them to the other vegetables and sauté for about 2 to 3 minutes.

Heat the rest of the oil in another pan and very briefly sear the chopped meat in small portions at high heat. Add to the vegetables.

Mince the ham and add it to the vegetables. Season with the salt, pepper, and herbs. Mix well and pour in the meat broth. Braise the ground-meat mixture at low heat for about 30 minutes.

Remove the mixture from the stove, cool slightly, stir in the egg. Cool completely.

Rub the inside of a large casserole with butter. Preheat the oven to 425°F (220°C). Stuff the cooked squares of dough with the cold ground-meat mixture, roll them up, and place in layers in the casserole. Pour the sour cream over the cannelloni, sprinkle with the grated cheese, and dot with butter.

Bake on the middle rack of the oven for 15 to 20 minutes or until crust is golden brown.

Macaroni and Eggplant Casserole

Maccheroni con le melanzane

They make this dish in the south of Italy. Although the ingredients vary, they always include eggplant and macaroni.

For 4 servings
2¹/₄ pounds (1 kg) eggplants
¹/₂ cup (125 mL) olive oil
salt
freshly ground white pepper
1 clove garlic
2 tablespoons vegetable oil
1 can (1 lb/500 g) peeled tomatoes
8 ounces (200 g) boiled ham
4 ounces (100 g) pecorino cheese plus ¹/₂ cup (50 g) grated pecorino
8 ounces (200 g) cooked boneless chicken
1 cup (100 g) shelled fresh peas
12 ounces (300 g) macaroni
2 tablespoons chopped fresh parsley
1 tablespoon chopped fresh basil

Wash the eggplants, remove the stems, and slice crosswise into slices about ¹/₈ inch (¹/₂ cm) thick. Line a large bowl with the slices and pour the olive oil on top. Sprinkle with the salt and pepper. Peel the garlic and force it through a press, onto the eggplant. Let the eggplant marinate about 30 minutes.

Heat the oil in a saucepan. Drain the tomatoes and sauté them about 15 minutes.

Dice the ham, cheese, and chicken and mix into the tomatoes along with the peas. Remove the pot from the stove.

Cook the macaroni in plenty of salted water for about 10 minutes, then drain and rinse with cold water.

Put the pasta in a large bowl and add the tomato mixture. Season with the salt, parsley, and basil and mix thoroughly.

Preheat the oven to 400°F (200°C). Line the bottom and sides of a large casserole with the marinated eggplant. Fill with the macaroni-tomato mixture. Cover the surface with the rest of the eggplant and sprinkle with the grated pecorino. Bake on the middle rack of the oven for 20 to 25 minutes or until bubbly.

Variation
Beef and Macaroni Casserole

Proceed as in the above recipe but use 1 pound (400 g) of mixed ground beef instead of the ham and chicken. Sear the meat in the oil at high heat while stirring constantly for about 5 minutes until the meat is very brown. Add the tomatoes and boil vigorously about 15 minutes. Add the cheese and continue as in the recipe for macaroni and Eggplant Casserole.

STUFFED PASTAS

Ravioli Stuffed with Lamb
Ravioli ripieni di agnello

For 4 servings
Dough
2¹/₄ cups (300 g) all-purpose flour
1 teaspoon salt
3 large eggs
2 tablespoons oil
Filling
3 tablespoons olive oil
¹/₂ clove garlic
1 medium onion
10 ounces (300 g) ground lamb
¹/₂ cup (125 mL) beef broth
¹/₂ teaspoon salt
freshly ground black pepper
pinch of freshly grated nutmeg
4-6 chopped fresh sage leaves
¹/₂ teaspoon each chopped fresh rosemary and thyme
1 tablespoon chopped fresh parsley
1 egg white, lightly beaten
¹/₃ cup (80 g) butter
³/₄ (80 g) freshly grated parmesan cheese

Make a pasta dough as described on page 41. Wrap in foil or plastic and let it rest for an hour in the refrigerator.

Heat the oil in a pan. Force garlic through a press. Mince the onion and sauté it and the garlic lightly in the oil. Add the lamb and brown it at high heat, turning constantly. Pour in the beef broth and season with the salt, pepper, nutmeg, sage, rosemary, thyme, and parsley. Simmer the lamb mixture about 20 minutes at medium heat, adding a little more broth if necessary. Let the lamb mixture cool.

Divide the dough into 4 equal portions. Roll out 2 portions into two 12-inch (32-cm) squares on a floured surface. Reserve the other portions in the refrigerator until ready to use.

Press straight lines into each square of dough with the back of a knife, making a grid of 2-inch (4-cm) squares. Place a tablespoon of filling in the middle of each small square and brush the spaces in between with beaten egg white. Cover with the second large square and press the lines forming the edges of the small squares firmly together with a strip of wood or a ruler. Pierce any bubbles with a pin. Cut the dough into squares with a pastry wheel. Proceed similarly with the remaining portions of dough.

Cook the ravioli in vigorously boiling salted water for about 12 to 15 minutes. Remove cooked ravioli and drain well.

Melt the butter in a pot and toss the drained ravioli in it. Serve with the grated cheese.

Variation
Ravioli with Ricotta and Wild Herbs

Season 10 ounces (300 g) ricotta or well-drained dry cottage cheese with salt and pepper and stir in 1 egg and a handful of wild herbs (the choice of herbs is left up to you).

This ravioli is also tossed with fresh butter and sprinkled with grated parmesan or grana padano.

Tortellini Stuffed with Meat

Tortellini con maiale

For 4 servings
Dough
2¹/₄ cups (300 g) all-purpose flour
1 teaspoon salt
3 large eggs
2 tablespoons oil
Filling
8 ounces (250 g) spinach
6 ounces (200 g) ground pork
6 ounces (200 g) cottage or ricotta cheese
1 cup (100 g) freshly grated parmesan cheese
1 large egg
¹/₂ teaspoon salt
freshly ground black pepper
pinch of freshly grated nutmeg
¹/₂ clove garlic, crushed
1 egg white, lightly beaten

To make the dough, sift the flour out onto a working surface, make a depression in the middle, and put the salt, egg, and oil in the depression. Mix into a firm and easy-to-knead dough. Cover with foil or plastic and let it rest at least an hour.

To make the filling, pick through the spinach, blanch briefly in salted water, and mince. Mix into a smooth paste with the pork, cottage cheese or ricotta, parmesan, egg, salt, pepper, nutmeg, and garlic.

Roll out the dough as thin as possible, let it relax for a while, and then cut into squares 2 to 3 inches (5 to 6 cm) wide. Put ¹/₂ teaspoon of filling on top of each square, fold into a triangle, and press the edges together firmly. To make the dough stick together better, brush the edges with a little beaten egg white. Roll the triangles over the tips of the fingers, pressing them together into rings. Let dry 1 to 2 hours.

Cook the tortellini in salted water for 12 minutes. Drain in a sieve and serve with freshly made tomato sauce (p. 64) and freshly grated parmesan cheese.

Tortellini Stuffed with Cheese

Tortellini ripieni di formaggio

This variation on tortellini is especially common in the Emilia Romagna region and takes its special flavor from the mixture of ricotta and garlic.

8 ounces (250 g) ricotta or drained cottage cheese
¹/₂ cup (50 g) freshly grated parmesan cheese
1 clove garlic, crushed
¹/₂ tablespoon chopped fresh basil
1 large egg
¹/₂ teaspoon salt
freshly ground white pepper
¹/₂ cup (115 g) butter, melted until lightly browned; or ¹/₂ cup (75 g) bread crumbs lightly browned in ¹/₄ cup (60 g) butter

Make the tortellini shells as described in the preceding recipe.

To make the filling, mash the ricotta thoroughly with a fork and mix into a smooth paste with the other ingredients. Cook in vigorously boiling water for 10 to 12 minutes; drain thoroughly.

Pour lightly browned butter over the cooked tortellini or sprinkle with bread crumbs browned in butter.

Spinach-Stuffed Tortelloni

Tortelloni di magro

For 4 to 6 servings
Dough
2¹/₄ cups (300 g) all-purpose flour
1 teaspoon salt
3 large eggs
2 tablespoons olive oil
Filling
2 pounds (750 g) Swiss chard; or 1 pound (500 g) young spinach
2 ounces (60 g) bacon
1 cup (225 g) butter
1 teaspoon salt
8 ounces (200 g) ricotta or dry cottage cheese
1 large egg
freshly ground black pepper
freshly grated nutmeg
1¹/₂ cups (150 g) freshly grated parmesan cheese; parmesan cheese for garnish
1 egg white, lightly beaten

Sift the flour onto a working surface, make a depression in the middle, and put in the salt, eggs, and olive oil. Make into a firm and easy to knead dough. Cover with foil or plastic wrap; refrigerate and let it rest at least an hour.

Wash the chard or spinach, removing the coarser chard stems, and cook for 5 to 8 minutes in plenty of salted water. Drain well.

Chop the bacon very fine and brown rapidly in a heavy skillet. Add 3 tablespoons (50 g) butter, let it brown, and swirl the chard or spinach through it. Put in a bowl, add the salt, ricotta or cottage cheese, egg, seasonings, and 1¹/₂ cups of parmesan cheese. Mix well and set aside.

Roll out the dough very thin and slice into 2- to 3-inch (5- to 6-cm) squares. Put the filling on top with a teaspoon, being careful to keep the edges of the dough clear.

To make the dough stick together especially well, brush beaten egg white around the edges. Fold the squares into triangles with peaks that do not overlap precisely, making two peaks. Press the edges together carefully to keep filling from leaking out while cooking. Brush a little egg white on the two upper peaks and press them together firmly.

Cook the tortelloni in plenty of salted water for about 15 to 20 minutes, then drain.

Brown the remaining butter and pour it over the tortelloni. Sprinkle with remaining grated parmesan.

Variation
Tortelloni with Spicy Filling

Use the dough from the preceding recipe and substitute this filling.

Filling
10 ounces (300 g) ricotta or cottage cheese
2 large eggs
¹/₂ teaspoon salt
freshly ground white pepper
1 teaspoon ground dried red pepper (cayenne)
4 ounces (150 g) fine-grained salami
1 fresh hot red pepper, cored and minced
¹/₂ medium onion
1 clove garlic

Press the liquid out of the cheese with a fork and mix in the eggs, salt, and white and ground red pepper well. Mince and add the salami and minced fresh red pepper. Mince the onion and stir into the cheese mixture. Peel the garlic and force through a press into the cheese.

Proceed as in the previous recipe and serve again with browned butter and a lot of grated parmesan cheese.

SOME MARVELOUS PASTA SALADS

Pasta Salad
Insalata di pasta

A pasta salad is a complete summer meal: a dish that satisfies though it is light and refreshing. Be as creative as possible and choose your ingredients according to your preferences. Salads call for pastas with plenty of body, such as macaroni, penne, shells, and rigatoni.

For 4 servings
10 ounces (300 g) tortiglioni
salt
6 tablespoons (90 mL) extra-virgin olive oil
4 tablespoons (60 mL) high-quality white-wine vinegar
juice of 1/2 lemon
3 tablespoons white wine
1 clove garlic
1/4 teaspoon freshly ground white pepper
2 tablespoons chopped fresh salad herbs
1/2 medium onion
4 small spring onions or scallions
2 small carrots
1 red bell pepper
1/2 cup (60 g) shelled small peas
8 ounces (250 g) mortadella

Cook the pasta in salted water until al dente—for 8 to 12 minutes, depending on the shape. Drain well. Mix the oil, vinegar, lemon juice, and wine in a large salad bowl. Press the garlic into the bowl and stir it in with a pinch of salt, pepper, and herbs.

Slice the spring onions into short sections. Scrape the carrots, blanch them briefly in salted water, and slice them crosswise. Cut the whole pepper in half, remove the seeds and ribs, and slice into strips. Add these vegetables to the dressing along with the peas. Cut the mortadella sausage into small cubes and add. Mix thoroughly. Stir in the cooked cold pasta, and let the salad marinate for 30 minutes in the refrigerator before serving.

Variation
Pasta Salad with Cheese

For 4 servings
10 ounces (300 g) penne, rigatoni, or shells
salt
2 tablespoons olive oil
juice of 1 lemon
2 tablespoons crème fraîche or heavy cream
1/4 teaspoon freshly ground white pepper
1 tablespoon chopped fresh chives
1 tablespoon chopped fresh parsley
2 medium onions
4 ounces (150 g) salami
8 ounces (250 g) asiago or tilsit cheese
1 green bell pepper

Cook the pasta in plenty of salted water until al dente, then drain and rinse with cold water. Mix the olive oil, lemon juice, and crème fraîche. Stir in a pinch of salt, pepper, and chopped herbs.

Peel and dice the onions. Dice the salami. Remove the rind from the asiago and slice the cheese into slender strips. Clean and finely chop the pepper. Add these ingredients to the dressing, stirring in well. Taste and adjust the seasonings. Toss dressing with pasta mixture. Let the salad marinate 30 minutes before serving.

Penne Salad with Tomatoes

Insalata di penne e pomodori

For 4 to 6 servings
10 ounces (300 g) penne rigate
salt
3 medium tomatoes
4 tablespoons (60 mL) oil
2 tablespoons balsamic vinegar
2 tablespoons dry white wine
1 bunch spring onions or scallions
2 tablespoons chopped fresh salad herbs
freshly ground white pepper
1/4 teaspoon sugar
1/2 teaspoon hot mustard
1/2 clove garlic
1/2 medium onion

Cook the pasta in plenty of salted water until *al dente*. Drain well. Let cool.

Cut the tomatoes into chunks. Mix the oil, vinegar, and wine in a large bowl. Slice the spring onions thin and add along with the herbs, salt, pepper, sugar, and mustard. Force the garlic through a press. Mince the onion and add it and the garlic.

Add the pasta and tomatoes, toss well, and chill before serving.

Tuna Salad with Shells

Conchiglie in insalata col tonno

For 4 servings
10 ounces (300 g) conchiglie
2 medium onions
1/2 cup (125 mL) beef broth, heated to boiling
4 artichoke hearts
2 cups (4 oz/100 g) tuna packed in oil
juice of 1 lemon
2 tablespoons olive oil
1/2 teaspoon salt
freshly ground white pepper

Cook the pasta in plenty of salted water until *al dente*. Drain and let cool. Mince the onions. Place in a large bowl and pour the hot meat broth over them. Mince the artichoke hearts and add them. Drain the tuna well, break it apart, and add to the salad bowl. Season with the lemon juice, olive oil, salt, and pepper. Toss well, mixing in the pasta, and marinate, covered, for at least an hour in the refrigerator before serving.

GNOCCHI AND POLENTA

Spinach Gnocchi
Gnocchi de spinaci

Although gnocchi are certainly pasta, they are hardly noodles. Nor are they like german-style dumplings. They are so interesting you can serve them as a main dish or a first course.

For 4 servings
1¹/₂ pounds (700 g) fresh spinach
salt
¹/₂ cup (115 g) butter
6 ounces (200 g) ricotta or dry cottage cheese
³/₄ cup (80 g) freshly grated parmesan cheese
freshly ground black pepper
pinch of freshly grated nutmeg
2 large eggs
³/₄ cup (100 g) all-purpose flour

Pick through and wash the spinach; remove the stems. Bring 2 tablespoons salted water to a boil, and steam the spinach just until it breaks up. Drain and chop it coarse. Melt 2 tablespoons (30 g) butter in a large saucepan, add the spinach and braise at medium heat until it is soft and the liquid has boiled away.

Add the ricotta or cottage cheese, ¹/₃ cup (40 g) parmesan, and the seasonings, followed by the eggs and flour. Mix thoroughly and let stand covered for about an hour in a cool place.

Bring large pot of salted water to a boil, then reduce heat so that the water simmers. Scoop small balls from the cooled dough with a teaspoon, slip them into the simmering water, and simmer—don't boil—about 7 minutes, until they feel firm. Remove with a skimmer, drain well, and keep warm. Put half of the remaining butter in a casserole and melt it. Add the gnocchi, sprinkle with remaining grated cheese, and dot with the rest of the butter. Bake at 400°F (200°C) until the cheese melts.

Potato Gnocchi
Gnocchi di patate

For 4 servings
2 pounds (800 g) cooled boiled potatoes
2¹/₄ cups (300 g) all-purpose flour
2 cups (200 g) freshly grated parmesan cheese
1 large egg yolk
1 teaspoon salt
freshly ground white pepper
¹/₄ cup (60 g) butter
1 clove garlic, crushed
2 tablespoons chopped fresh parsley
¹/₂ teaspoon each chopped fresh rosemary, mint, thyme, and oregano

1 cup (100 g) freshly grated parmesan cheese

Peel the potatoes and force them through a ricer. Distribute the potatoes over a working surface. Put the flour, parmesan cheese, egg yolk, salt, and pepper on top. Knead into a soft but plastic dough and let rest about an hour in a cool place.

Boil a sample dumpling first. If the dough is too soft, add a little flour or farina. Shape into a roll of dough about as thick as your thumb and cut into sections about 1 inch (3 cm) long. Roll these into balls and flatten them slightly with a fork. Simmer these gnocchi in salted boiling water for about 7 minutes, lift out and drain, and arrange them on hot plates.

Melt the butter, add the garlic and herbs, and spoon over the gnocchi. Serve with grated parmesan cheese on the side.

Polenta Gnocchi
Gnocchi di polenta

For 4 servings
2 cups (450 mL) water
1-1½ teaspooons salt
¾ cup (150 g) yellow cornmeal
Herb butter
⅓ cup (80 g) butter
2 fresh sage leaves
fresh rosemary, oregano, and lemon balm
1 cup (100 g) grated fontina cheese (optional)

Bring the water and salt to a boil in a large pot and stir in the cornmeal slowly, constantly beating with a whisk. When all the cornmeal is incorporated, stir the mixture with a wooden spatula over very low heat so that the meal can absorb the liquid and turn into polenta. Be careful to keep it from burning. A thin and light layer should form on the bottom of the pot. Pour the mush onto a wet wooden board or stone slab, press it down into a smooth sheet about ½ inch (1 cm) thick and let cool.

Melt the butter and mix with herbs. Preheat the oven to 425°F (220°C).

Cut the polenta into strips or use a cookie cutter for fancy shapes as desired. Place in layers in a wide, shallow casserole and pour the herb butter on top.

If desired, sprinkle fontina over the polenta. Bake gnocchi on the middle rack of the oven until the cheese melts, about 10 minutes.

Gnocchi Roman Style
Gnocchi alla romana

For 4 servings
2 cups (450 mL) milk
½ teaspoon salt
freshly grated nutmeg
¾ cup (150 g) farina
3 large eggs
¾ cup (80 g) freshly grated grana padano cheese
½ cup (100 g) butter, melted

Bring the milk to a boil with the salt and nutmeg. Add the farina all at once and simmer about 20 minutes, stirring constantly with a whisk. Remove from the heat and cool a little.

Whip the eggs and stir into the slightly cooled farina. Mix well.

Rinse a baking sheet with cold water and with a spatula spread a layer of cooked farina about ⅛ inch (½ cm) thick on it. Let it cool completely, preferably in the refrigerator. Cut the chilled farina into 2-inch (4-cm) circles.

Preheat the oven to 425°F (220°C). Generously butter an ovenproof casserole and arrange layers of gnocchi inside. Sprinkle grated cheese and pour melted butter over each layer. Bake until golden brown on the middle rack of the oven.

Variation
Gnocchi Bolognese

Polenta can also be placed in a casserole with the Bolognese Sauce (page 54), sprinkled with grated parmesan cheese, and baked at 425°F (220°C) until the cheese melts.

IMPORTANT ITALIAN CHEESES

Cheese is one of the most basic ingredients of pizza and of most pasta dishes. Although the hard varieties are especially used as seasoning, a wide range of soft cheeses are also employed, the most common being mozzarella.

1 Provolone

The well-aged 4-to-6-month-old cheese is especially pungent and appropriate for grating. Produced in various forms, usually kneaded into rolls or pear shapes. Also available smoked.

2 Grana padano

Indispensable for pastas. Closely related in shape, color, and flavor to parmesan although produced in northern Italy. This hard cheese is, when "vecchio" (fully ripe), ideal for grating and can be used exactly like parmesan.

3 Mozzarella

Genuine mozzarella will be labeled *di bufala* because it is made from buffalo milk. It is almost always used in pizzas as well as pasta dishes.

4 Fiore sardo

A piquant cheese made from sheep milk, good for grating and appropriate for many types of pasta.

5 Asiago

When really ripe this semisoft slicing cheese is also a piquant ingredient in pastas and an ideal topping for pizzas.

6 Fontina

A soft, mellow slicing cheese from Piedmont. It is used relatively young and fresh.

7 Taleggio

A high-fat soft cheese in a rectangular shape with an unmistakable pungent aroma. It lends pasta dishes an especially piquant flavor.

8 Gorgonzola

A bleu cheese made from cow's milk. Its sharp and unmistakable flavor and creamy consistency make it an ideal ingredient for piquant pastas.

9 and 10 Caciocavallo

A high-fat hard cheese in the shape of a pear or pouch, it is also available smoked. New caciocavallo (up to 6 months old) is a good pizza topping.

11 Parmigiano-reggiano

The most famous Italian hard cheese is parmigiano-reggiano. The ideal grating cheese for Italian pasta and risotto, it comes from the region of Emilia-Romagna. Only if it is made in the vicinity of the city of Parma can it be designated "parmigiano." Aged for two years, it develops its wonderfully pungent, rather nutty, taste and is used for grating or eaten as a snack with wine.

12 Robiola

A high-fat fresh cheese usually made from a mixture of cows', sheeps', and goats' milk, this fresh cheese is just one step past heavy cream. Although mild, it has a memorable flavor and is often marketed combined with fruits or spices.

13 Italico

A relative of robiola, thoroughly ripened and often crusted with mold. Pungent and piquant.

14 Pecorino

Not illustrated, but an important sheep-milk cheese for pastas. Depending on its provenance and age it can be mild or piquant.

METRIC—IMPERIAL CONVERSION TABLE

Note that the recipes in this book feature both U.S. customary and metric measurements. For cooks in Great Britain, Canada, and Australia, note the following information for imperial measurements. If you are familiar with metric measurements, then we recommend you follow those, incorporated into every recipe. If not, then use these conversions to achieve best results. Bear in mind that ingredients such as flour vary greatly and you will have to make some adjustments.

Liquid Measures

The British cup is larger than the American. The Australian cup is smaller than the British but a little larger than the American. Use the following cup measurements for liquids, making the adjustments as indicated.

U.S.	1 cup (236 ml)
British and Canadian	1 cup (284 ml)—adjust measurement to $1/4$ pint + 2 tablespoons
Australian	1 cup (250 ml)—adjust measurement to $1/4$ pint

Weight and Volume Measures

U.S. cooking procedures usually measure certain items by volume, although in other countries these items are often measured by weight. Here are some approximate equivalents for basic items.

	U.S. Customary	Metric	Imperial
Butter	1 cup	250 g	8 ounces
	$1/2$ cup	125 g	4 ounces
	$1/4$ cup	62 g	2 ounces
	1 tablespoon	15 g	$1/2$ ounce
Flour (sifted all-purpose or plain)	1 cup	128 g	$4^{1/4}$ ounces
	$1/2$ cup	60 g	$2^{1/8}$ ounces
	$1/4$ cup	32 g	1 ounce
Sugar (caster)	1 cup	240 g	8 ounces
	$1/2$ cup	120 g	4 ounces
	1 tablespoon	15 g	$1/2$ ounce
Chopped vegetables	1 cup	115 g	4 ounces
	$1/2$ cup	60 g	2 ounces
Chopped meats or fish	1 cup	225 g	8 ounces
	$1/2$ cup	110 g	4 ounces

INDEX

Christian Teubner is a highly sought-after photographer specializing in food photography. His work conveys the special magic and fun of cooking, whether he is picturing soups, main courses, or desserts. He again shows his love of cooking in this beautifully illustrated collection of his favorite recipes.